Find Your Way Through Divorce

Find Your Way
Through Divorce

Jill Curtis

Hodder & Stoughton
LONDON SYDNEY AUCKLAND

British Library Cataloguing in Publication Data
A record for this book is available from the British Library

ISBN 0 340 78587 X

Typeset by Avon Dataset Ltd, Bidford-on-Avon, Warks

Printed and bound in Great Britain by
The Guernsey Press Co. Ltd, Channel Isles

Hodder & Stoughton
A Division of Hodder Headline Ltd
338 Euston Road
London NW1 3BH

With love to all my family –
especially Matilda and Grace

'Love does not consist in gazing at each other, but in looking outward together in the same direction.'

ANTOINE DE SAINT-EXUPÉRY

Contents

Self-help checklists and questionnaires

Acknowledgments

My heartfelt thanks to my husband John. Not only for so many years of happy marriage but for his constant love and support. This book would not have been written without his encouragement and confidence in me. His wizardry on the computer and his editorial skills have truly underpinned it throughout.

I am extremely grateful to Judith Longman at Hodder & Stoughton for her enthusiasm right from the start, and to Rebecca Russel Ponte for her watchful eye during the whole editing and production processes.

Acknowledgements

Introduction

Love and marriage may well go together like a horse and carriage in songs and in our dreams but what happens when the road gets rough, the horse gets sick or the wheel comes off? There are so many hopes and dreams at the beginning for every couple who make a commitment to each other. There is a belief that 'love conquers all'. Unfortunately, this is not backed up by the statistics: they show that a high percentage of relationships break down. We are told that two out of three marriages fail, and this does not include the number of couples who cohabit and then part, since these are not recorded in the figures. Latest research shows children born to unmarried couples are twice as likely to see their parents split up. So why do so many people still promise to love each other, care for each other, and forsake all others 'Till death do us part'?

We are all happy enough to celebrate in public the union of two people in love. Yet, when and if they break up later, the tears are usually at first in private. A problem, if it does arise, may seem to be for the couple alone to sort out. However, if it causes a break-up, it soon spills over to involve the whole family and friends as well. We are all affected in one way or another by the difficulties and sadness of a broken marriage. Could this be one of the reasons why women, and quite a few men, find they have tears in their eyes at a wedding?

It can be a heart-wrenching moment to catch a glimpse of the love and trust which is there for all to see as vows are exchanged. We watch two people stepping out into the future together expecting to live happily ever after. Unfortunately, at most weddings today there is no fairy godmother to guarantee this will be so.

How is it that some couples can stay the course, and celebrate a long and happy life together? What is their secret or have they just been lucky? How is it that dark clouds can form so speedily over some relationships, followed by a breakdown of communication and ending in solicitors' letters and anger and blame all round?

Practically all marriages hit a rough patch sooner or later. Perhaps the real test of love and commitment comes then. This is a book about divorce; you may be reading it because you cannot decide if divorce is the right course for you to follow and you hope to prevent a final showdown. Perhaps at the moment you have more questions than you have answers. Maybe you are involved with someone who is already married, and wonder how the break-up of one relationship can actually take place in a way that makes the creation of a new partnership possible, not one haunted by guilt and contrition.

Does your partner want to leave you? How are you to deal with this and come out the other side? I go through the factors that can lead up to the decision to part, what it will mean, and how you and your partner will be affected. But this is not necessarily the only road to take, and hopefully your marriage can be saved. If so, I look at how you can decide what is right for you and how you and your partner can sort things out. On the other hand, for those of you who see no way of turning back and recapturing lost love, I hope this book will help you avoid the bitter recrimination which is so hurtful when divorce is inevitable. I suggest ways to ease the pain, not just to you and your partner but to the children as well, for they are so often the innocent victims who suffer most.

Whether you have been through a legal or religious marriage ceremony, or whether you and your partner have made a private commitment to each other, you are a couple. The 2001 census for the first time invited people to classify themselves as 'partner' as an alternative to 'husband' or 'wife'. Today there are many different combinations which constitute a family, so although I use the word 'marriage' in this book for the sake of clarity and simplicity, I am referring to partnerships of all kinds; when I use the word 'partner' it would be just as appropriate for me to use 'husband' or 'wife'. I also use 'he' and 'she' where each seems most appropriate, but they are almost always interchangeable. I hope the reader will accept that this does not reflect a masculine or feminine bias.

Part One

The End of Your Marriage?

In matrimony, to hesitate is sometimes to be saved.
(Samuel Butler)

1

Bringing things to a head

I hope and I believe that I am speaking for both of us when I say we think married life is wonderful and hope we will be spared to enjoy it for a very long time to come.

(Prince Andrew just after his wedding)

Is your relationship breaking down?

Today none of us can afford to be complacent about our own marriage. Will yours survive? Or will you be one of the ever-growing number of couples who face the breakdown of their partnership? Although marriage is still very much in fashion and the number of couples prepared to make a commitment to each other has remained constant for the past few years, very many of the promises get broken sooner or later.

How can the starry-eyed bride or groom be expected to pause and reflect on the pitfalls which may lie ahead? Do you remember how, when you fell in love, you believed that you and your loved one could face the world together whatever happened? Can you recall the promises you made to each other? Do you remember the feeling of having wings on your heels and the way that romance seemed to be all around you?

Being 'in love' brings with it many powerful emotions. To feel in tune with another person can help us to feel truly alive and authentic, as if we have been validated as an individual. The strange thing about love is that whereas we can usually pinpoint the moment when we said to ourselves (and to our partner) 'I'm in love', there is often no precise moment when we begin to realize that that love is no longer there; the awareness of falling out of love is a gradual process.

Love is a state of mind and feeling. It goes hand in hand with liking, respect, shared interests, trust and a degree of idealization. A romance based on fantasies alone cannot last, and this accounts for many short-term relationships. So what is love and what is lust? The happiest of couples share a degree of both.

Are you wondering if your relationship is heading for the rocks? Is your relationship in trouble? Too many partnerships founder because neither of the partners takes responsibility for ensuring that the relationship doesn't drift into those dangerous waters which might be labelled 'apathy' or 'indifference'. Has this happened to you? Relationships need taking care of and lucky are the couples who instinctively know this from the beginning and successfully navigate through choppy waters. On the other hand, there can, of course, be cataclysmic events which bring about the end of a marriage all too suddenly. What if you are told by your partner that you are no longer loved or wanted? This can be a soul-destroying moment, and one you feel you may never recover from.

> *'I think my marriage is in trouble, but my partner doesn't seem to be worrying.'*

How do you know if there are difficulties in your marriage?

First of all, what is it about your relationship which is making you uneasy? Is it just that things aren't what they used to be? Or is it more than that?

You should be aware that all relationships have rough patches. That's life. And anyone who believes that marriage means living happily ever after is in for a big surprise. The starry-eyed bride and groom can't possibly know whether physical or mental illness, financial hardship, abuse or just neglect will be the assailant of their happiness. The pressures of everyday life are extreme today. So once the honeymoon period is over getting through the day and all that that entails – pressures at work, problems at home, even financial worries – uses up a lot of energy. This may mean that you have too little time left to work at your marriage, and you have begun to take your partner for granted. This is a very easy trap to fall into. Have you stopped doing those little things for each other which make you feel loved? You know what I mean: that cold drink brought out when your partner is into DIY, or the spontaneous neck rub when you are at your most tense. Small things in themselves, but they all add to the amount of treasure in the emotional marital bank.

Has this happened to you? If it has, it is not easy to regain the comfortable and loving relationship you had in the past. It may not be easy, but it is not impossible either.

Signs that your relationship is in trouble:

- Are you feeling lost? As if you have arrived at a destination with no idea of how you got there, or which route to take now?
- Have you lost that feeling of well-being and contentment without being certain why?

- Have you already found yourself wondering if, given your choice over again, you would have married the same person?
- Have you found that you have stopped taking into account your partner's feelings when you make a decision?
- Are you no longer in love?

If you answered 'yes' more often than 'no' to these questions, you should be aware that alarm bells have started to ring!

Is there still trust in your relationship?

The skill in keeping in step with your partner is often to be alert to dangers within and outside the marriage. For any couple there must be a degree of trust in the relationship. This trust can be broken when the first unexpected physical or emotional blow is struck, like the discovery of undisclosed debts. But most likely it is suspicion of infidelity which brings doubt into the relationship. This jealousy, for that is what it is, gnaws away at any peace of mind. But, if you jumped to the conclusion that 'something was up' every time your partner was half an hour late or the telephone was hung up whenever *you* answered it, it would not make for a comfortable partnership, or life.

'How could I have been so blind? All the signs were there now I look back. Do you think he wanted me to know right from the beginning that he was having an affair?'

We all need to know that we can believe in our partner and count on his or her loyalty. After all, wasn't this what you promised each other when you made a commitment to become a couple? When we are in a happy and close partnership, it reinforces the confidence we have in ourselves, and each other. You are pleased that your partner has close friends, and that you both can chat to other people at a party, safe in the knowledge that your loyalty to each other is not in question. But when the most intimate relationship becomes shaky or when there is danger in the air, this affects our own estimation of ourselves, and can attack our confidence, and our sense of security, at a stroke.

Is there cheating going on?

There are many reasons why a couple can find themselves in difficulties, and one of the most common is when a third person becomes entangled in their lives. We have all heard the saying, 'The wife (or husband) is always the last to know' and indeed this is almost always so when one's partner is involved with someone else. This isn't to say that somewhere deep inside yourself you may not have had an idea that *something* was happening, but an instinctive mechanism of self-protection comes into action so that we do not allow our suspicions to penetrate our conscious thought. 'Adultery' and 'infidelity' are ugly words and it is just too painful to stomach the fact that your partner is betraying you.

George had been married for seven years when his world crashed around his ears. 'I had no idea there was any trouble between us until she told me she had found someone else.' How could it have happened that a couple living together, even happily according to George, could at the same time be so far apart that it was possible for another person to become more important to his wife than George was himself? How could he 'not have known'? And yet this happens all the time.

Linda had been with her partner for over ten years when the ground went from under her feet: 'I can honestly say that it came out of the blue when he said he wanted to leave me.' However, Linda went on to say that for at least two years she had felt depressed. She was conscious of a feeling of lassitude and blamed herself for her inability to become interested in everyday things. She had even thought of seeing her doctor and asking for some medication to 'buck her up'. But once she heard from her husband about his three-year affair, she began to see that she had in fact been reacting to a very real danger, although she was not able to identify it for what it was at the time. Linda felt a whole range of emotions. Anger and fury were the main ones: she was enraged that for the past couple of years she had blamed herself for feeling so unsure about herself; she was incensed that she had felt unhappy and unresponsive to her husband's half-hearted attempts to make love. Once the affair was in the open, Linda felt she could fight back, but she still continued to blame herself for not speaking up earlier when she had sensed something was happening which didn't feel right. Her anger towards her husband was fuelled by her memory of berating herself for not satisfying him in the way she had done in earlier days.

What signs might George and Linda have looked for? Why should you doubt that your partner was where he said he would be? How is it that you can trick yourself into believing otherwise? How many times can you give your partner the benefit of the doubt when sex is avoided because of a 'headache' or 'pressure of work'? Can you really have accepted that his increased irritability and lack of interest in your home life were caused by something you were or were not doing?

Ask yourself if he is facing the age-old dilemma of a straying partner: fretting about how a new relationship can feel so right when he is with his mistress, but so wrong when at home with his family.

A word of caution: don't jump to conclusions too soon. Make sure your partner isn't struggling with external issues, such as a recent bereavement, threat of job loss or redundancy. Take a moment to check that he is not suffering from depression or a physical illness.

A partner's infidelity – the signs to look for:

- **Evasiveness and lies** Have you noticed your partner being 'economical with the truth' – or found him out in a lie?
- **Irritability** Has your partner been quite snappy lately for no obvious reason?
- **Mood swings** Have you noticed unexplained changes of mood? Perhaps 'over happy' at times, and at other times very depressed, even tearful?
- **General air of discontentment** Have you been aware of an air of dissatisfaction around – nothing enjoyed quite so much as earlier, or little enthusiasm for things you used to do together?
- **Increased or decreased sexual activity** Has there been a change in your love-making recently? Is it suddenly more frequent, or different? Or has it stopped altogether?
- **Avoidance of time spent together** Does your partner go out of his way not to be alone with you?
- **Sudden 'overkill' of attention** Have you been overwhelmed by sudden attention and treats?
- **Changes of habit** Has your partner taken up a new activity (which excludes you) or even started wearing new and different underwear?

'Killing you softly with his words'

Some men and women get worked up with rage when they realize they have been lulled into a false sense of security by their partners being more cheerful and sex seeming better with even a new, exciting dimension added. If they tentatively brought up the subject of their anxieties, they may even have been mocked or laughed at for their fears and lovingly reassured that all was well. It is not unusual for the unfaithful spouse to pay *more* attention to their partner in the hope that an illicit affair will not be discovered. This is a convenient way of averting suspicion and covering over clues which are often there to behold. It opens the way for the illusion that 'My affair improved my marriage'.

On the other hand there are some men and women who, whether consciously or not, *want* the affair to be discovered and it is then that clues are left around to be discovered supposedly 'unintentionally'. A discarded receipt for dinner for two or a hotel bill left in the pocket of a suit for the cleaners may often be a way of forcing into the open an issue which it has been impossible to discuss. This is a way of causing the *other* to say, 'What is going on?' or even to ask, 'Is there someone else?' Recently, with so many mobile phones in use, I have heard of the itemized telephone bill being left in a prominent place 'by mistake' for this purpose. The most stalwart unconscious defences are breached when faced with a bill showing daily lengthy telephone calls to a number you cannot identify. Equally, the e-mails in the personal filing cabinet on a laptop can bring about a confrontation earlier than anticipated. When the news of an affair finally breaks into the open, the first words often are, 'I *knew* something was up'. It can be like a bright light being turned on after you have been kept in the dark, which of course you have. Suddenly all those half suspicions or unexplained events can be seen for what they were.

I wonder what the word 'affair' suggests to you? Maybe it conjures up a mental picture of romance and intrigue. On the other hand you may know that it is more likely to mean broken hearts and grief. It all depends on where you are standing. Are you part of a previously committed couple, or a third person trying to get in and break it up? There is no way that everyone is going to be a winner when the battle is over.

> *'We were fine at the beginning of our affair. In a perfect bubble. It was only when the outside world came crashing in that all the pain was felt.'*

Perhaps you are involved in a triangle of this kind and you wonder which way to jump? If you are a woman involved with a married man, the danger is that you will slip into a dead-end relationship which may spoil your chances of eventually finding that special someone who will be with you always (over the holidays and weekends too!). What often begins with a buzz and thrill can soon pall when there is little sign that the man you are sleeping with is going to have the courage to choose you.

On the other hand, up to now you may have been in a partnership and you are the one to stray. The decision to stay or leave is so devastating that you find it hard to believe that at the start of your affair you were unaware of what lay ahead. So pause a moment and consider why you have become involved with someone else.

A dilemma, all too frequent, is when two people who are both married have an affair and in time decide they must be together always. Pillow talk can be very different from reality: one of the lovers may split from his family only to discover that his lover has had a change of heart and can't find the courage to leave her husband and children. You should be aware that it needs a streak of ruthlessness to break up a family however it is functioning and even though it may not be perfect.

'I thought I'd go mad. I broke up my family and still Len said he couldn't do the same. We had agreed! He said he needed more time. "Time for what?" I screamed at him.'

'Justin said his wife and kids hadn't done anything wrong so how could he go home and tell them he was leaving?'

'I really did believe him when he said his marriage was over and that we would be together. I couldn't understand how it could be so hard for him to leave. Eventually, I had to walk away from him. It was the hardest thing I have ever done.'

Why do people have affairs?

There are as many answers to this question as there are couples. But the lure of the forbidden can be a strong aphrodisiac. To be involved in a clandestine relationship can bring with it a heightened sexuality that you may not have felt for years. The secret meetings and messages, together with the belief that you are getting away with something, may seem like a lot of fun. At first, at any rate. At the beginning of an affair you may feel more attractive than you have for a long time.

> 'This may sound silly but when Harry started flirting with me, I didn't know how to handle it. All I knew was that it was a great morale booster and I began to feel better about myself. The tears came later.'

Whether you are the one tempted to stray, or the one who is left behind, the wise thing to do is to ask yourself *why*? *Why* has such a thing happened to you both? You may have believed that 'All you need is love, love' but you should also have learnt that love is *not* enough, and to keep a relationship healthy and alive needs more input of other kinds from both partners.

Is boredom or restlessness a sufficient reason to bring about the collapse of a marriage? If you feel that you are heading this way, think long and hard about it. If you change one partner for another without understanding what has brought this about, who is to say whether or not the same scenario will be repeated in a few years? You will be well advised to think about what it is that your new love does for you that your present partner does not. Is it because you have never asked or indicated in any way that there is something more you need from the relationship? Do you want to be more adventurous in bed? Do you want to talk more about the way you feel? Do you want to fulfill a secret dream before it is too late? Are you angry about the way your life is panning out? What makes you think that your present partner might not be harbouring these thoughts too?

> *'My sister was killed, and Stephen hardly spoke to me about it at all. My affair with Nigel began when he asked me if I wanted to have a drink and talk about her death. We talked for hours. It went on from there.'*

Before we consider the broad categories into which most affairs fall, it must be acknowledged that for one partner to be involved with 'someone else' there must be something missing in the relationship. This is often a very painful pill to swallow, but it is true to say that no third person can get into a relationship if there is not a void somewhere.

Affairs – ask yourself if any of these fit the bill:

- **Loneliness** Has the easy companionship gone out of your relationship?
- **Restlessness** Are either of you seeking a new way of life? Or sensing that your life together is in a rut?
- **Fear of ageing** Is there a nagging anxiety about getting older? Less fit?
- **Searching for sexual fulfilment** Have you or your partner been dissatisfied with your sexual relationship?
- **Inability to form lasting relationships** Do either of you find it hard to sustain long term relationships? Do you feel people always let you down?
- **Lack of commitment** Is it hard to keep up your obligations?

Main reasons for affairs

- ### *The inability to maintain a healthy adult relationship*
  Most people who have been habitually unfaithful to their partners may not like to acknowledge that this is the true reason.
  The wonderful feeling of falling in love goes on forever only in
  fairy tales; in real life this feeling gradually changes and needs to
  merge into a mature kind of loving. Remember that when we
  fall head over heels in love we are yearning for the kind of ideal
  partner we want to find, truly 'the other half', who will make us
  feel whole. In reality, when we get to know, *really* know, that
  other person we have to alter our conception to encompass our
  lover's own identity. If we are unable to do this, the temptation is
  to move on and find another person we believe fits the picture,
  the dream, we hold in our minds. This quest can become
  addictive.

---

*'I suppose I do fall in love easily, but I can't count the number of
disappointing relationships I have had. I think it's the men who
put on a front, until you get to know them that is.'*

- ### *'I didn't mean it to happen'*
  Too often I have heard these words as a justification for the
  turmoil which follows. Often a future liaison begins unexpectedly
  with a shared laugh, or a joint project: James told me that
  working closely with Linda, and enjoying it, made him suddenly
  realize he couldn't remember the last time he had felt so in tune
  with someone. 'It hit me how lonely I was. My wife and I had
  stopped communicating, and I had no idea of what she was
  thinking any more.' A thrill of adventure, the secrecy, the excitement of pulling the wool over everybody's eyes can seem fun at
  first, but no relationship stays the same, and sooner or later one
  or the other wants to change the rules. That is when the fat is in
  the fire; it is time to accept that someone will get badly burnt.

> *'I found someone who spoke the same language, I couldn't believe what a relief it was.'*

- ### You are knocked sideways by the arrival on the scene of an uninhibited and predatory man or woman

  A strong mutual sexual attraction can bring two people unexpectedly together. Perhaps you have always had a secret wish to be swept off your feet, and a man with a strong sexual drive becomes the knight who is able to carry you away. His sexuality may take you into newly discovered country, but there is often a very high price to pay for this, especially if sexual attraction and desire is mistaken for love and the 'real thing'. If a husband or wife is discarded for this reason alone, the bombshell waiting to explode may be the discovery that you don't even *like* the new lover . . . out of bed, that is. So beware.

> *'I was happy enough for four years with Joe, then wham! Brian literally swept me off my feet. We met on a bus of all places. Within two hours we were in bed together. I had no idea sex could be like that. Six months later I had lost Joe and Brian.'*

- ### 'Mid-life crisis'

  Too often we hear about a 'mid-life crisis'. What exactly is this? There may be a wish to hold back the tide of ageing: an attempt – almost never outwardly acknowledged – to regain the joy of youth by finding a younger partner. Although this may seem faintly ridiculous to friends and family, we all know of men who feel their wives of many years no longer 'suit'; this desire to have a second chance is at the root of many infidelities. This agenda is no longer limited to men only. Women now feel able to take up with much younger men, but the odds are still stacked against women because the biological clock ticks for them, and no one has found a way of putting that on hold.

• *A family crisis*

Trouble in the world outside your immediate relationship may well cause a very real difficulty in your marriage. As hard as it may be to accept this, the death of a parent, or a child, or a miscarriage, a job loss, or even inability to conceive may be enough to drive a wedge between a couple. All too often when it is a time to pull together, one of the partners turns for comfort to someone else. It could be that you felt it would be too painful to discuss the matter with each other, even from fear of making the hurt worse. But what could hurt your partner more than to know you have sought solace in another's arms?

'I didn't feel fifty years old – more like thirty. I was too young to be a grandfather and Lily gave me another chance to be a dad. Only Lily understood why I left my wife, no one else seemed to.'

• *'Coming out'*

An increasing number of men and women, who after being part of a heterosexual relationship for years and possibly being a parent too, find they have denied their sexuality for too long, so they 'come out' as gay or lesbian, no matter what the consequences. Some couples are torn apart by this revelation. Not so for all, though, and where love runs deep it is possible for this tragedy to be faced together. I use the word 'tragedy' for that is what it is. To live 'underground' for years, perhaps not consciously knowing the cause of an underlying grief, can be a torture. Just as it can be to discover that the person you love most in the world has kept this secret from you and you have to accept a completely different view of your partner, and in some cases the shattering realization that you have lost him to a new partner of his own sex.

'I would never have let myself even think I was gay all those years ago. Then I met someone who made me reconsider my whole life. Actually my husband was very loving and understanding once he got over the shock. We are still friends, but my children were less than understanding.'

'Try saying you were gay when I was a lad – no way. At sixty I got a chance of a new life, and took it.'

'Of course I was shocked when Clive told me he thought he was gay. We'd been married for thirty years. Yet, I soon saw he was the same man I loved before the bombshell hit me. I thought we would deal with it together. But that was not to be. He went on to say he had a new partner. I still love him.'

Is a break-up the only way forward?

What are you to do? The final piece of the jigsaw has been put into place, and it all makes horrible sense. Whether it is you or your partner who has brought matters to a head, you feel your relationship has reached a crisis point. YOU MUST THINK VERY CAREFULLY ABOUT WHAT YOUR NEXT MOVE SHOULD BE.

Do you really want to end your marriage? Is this the only solution? Would it be better or possible for you both to make compromises? There are men and women who stay in a marriage under the most appalling circumstances. Is boredom, a loveless or a sexless marriage, or even infidelity a reason to bring a marriage to an end? Take, for instance, Hillary Rodham Clinton: she has stayed in her marriage (much to the wrath of many women). She cites her strong sense of family, and her daughter, as the reasons.

If there has been an act of violence, drug or alcohol abuse once too often, endless broken promises or discovery of a sexual 'fling' it is understandable that you will want to declare this the end of the road. But this is not the time to draw up the battle lines. The danger is that all the resentment and hostility stored up over months, or even years, will come pouring out, and later you may regret things said and actions taken in the heat of the moment.

If there is a hope of staying together there is one other point to bear in mind: if you, too, have had an affair is it wise to tell your partner in a tit-for-tat way? If it is all over now, is it advisable to tell your partner what he may not have been aware of? Stop and think. What would be the reason to spill the beans now? You may trick yourself into believing that to clear the slate you need to confess to any and every misdemeanour, but more likely it is either revenge or to feel better yourself and have an easy conscience. So, although you may sleep better at night, it is likely that your partner, now in possession of all the facts, will have been pushed to the edge of another precipice and won't be able to pull back.

Talking to your partner

This may seem an obvious thing to do if your relationship is causing you any worry at all. And yet, the surprise is that many men and women do find this an awkward and difficult thing to do. It is okay to chat about events and everyday things, but areas where the emotions are involved seem to make even the most articulate fumble for words. 'Oh, I couldn't' and 'How would I even start?' are comments I have heard over and over again. It is as if words fail you when you attempt to find a common *emotional* language to express how you are feeling.

To say 'he wouldn't understand' is often a mask to cover up your own reluctance to find the words to talk things through. Is this something you have heard yourself say? How long is it since you and your partner had a real heart-to-heart talk? Possibly you can't even remember. This may mean that you and your partner are out of the habit of talking to each other, *really* talking. If this is the case then you will need to think very carefully before embarking on this track. Before you take this route you must be clear in your own mind what you want to talk about. It will not help either of you, or the relationship, if the tête-à-tête you are planning turns out to be another painful dialogue. Or even worse, a monologue where you find yourself listing your grievances one more time.

'I can feel her slipping away and I don't know what to do or say.'

Beware of just itemizing the things your partner has or hasn't done. It will be much more fruitful if you can find a way of explaining how you feel, and then leave the door open so as to listen to your partner's comments.

Once you have made up your mind about the points you want to discuss with your partner, find the right time to do this. Starting to have a serious talk just before friends are due to arrive, the children need feeding, or when you know your partner will be exhausted, will not help. It is essential to find the time when you are sure you will not be interrupted. If this is difficult to arrange, then take it upon yourself to *make* the time and space. Be sure that the time is right for you too. Avoid sticking to your plan if you are feeling under the weather or stressed. If you can be calm, and as relaxed as possible, then this will be transmitted to your partner. If you are on edge, this too will be conveyed and it will set off alarm bells. Not the best context for the fruitful discussion you are hoping to have.

Set the scene with care. Here is a checklist to help you plan the operation:

- Carefully plan in advance what you want to discuss with your partner. Be specific.
- Choose a good time to do this.
- Don't begin every sentence with 'YOU'. It sounds very aggressive.
- Try to talk about the way *you* see the situation.

- Give your partner the space to contribute his point of view. You may be surprised at what you hear!
- Be prepared to listen.

Once you are certain that you are in the right frame of mind, work out exactly what you want to talk about, then, when you feel the time is right, draw a deep breath and take the plunge. And don't forget to give your partner the opportunity to speak as well! Remember, you may only have one shot at this.

'I told her how unhappy I was, and she came right back and told me she was too . . . and was thinking of leaving me!'

'I didn't think through what I wanted to say, and it all came out as a jumble of complaints. Not what I meant to happen at all.'

'It came as a shock to us both to realize we had got out of the habit of talking and listening to each other.'

Perhaps the last point – listening – will be the hardest of all. You may have set the scene, even rehearsed what you want to say, but remember you may still be in for a shock. Your partner may believe that *you* have not picked up signals or messages in the past. So be prepared. It will be worth it.

When did the problems start?

When was the honeymoon over? Or did it never really start? It is always a shock to be told, or to feel, that things never were good. Is that your experience? Some couples can make a honeymoon last for years, and by that I mean they can learn to be in step and move easily from no longer being single to becoming a couple, a pair.

Other couples may feel that things never were right and even in those early days they were uneasy about the future together.

> *'A couple? Once the wedding was over I felt shackled to her.'*
>
> *'I woke up on my honeymoon and knew I had made a terrible mistake.'*

Should you confront your partner with your suspicions?

What if you feel the time for talking and discussion has passed, and that you have evidence you want to challenge your partner with? Again, it is important that you choose the right time. You may have an urge to humiliate or embarrass your partner, but it will not be helpful if, for instance, you appear at the office or any other public place and make a 'scene'. Confronting your partner head-on and asking the all-important question, 'Is there someone else?' is likely to bring any relationship to the brink of a crisis. If you have some proof of infidelity, and it is extraordinary how often firm evidence is available, then you already know the answer. Have you worked out what the next step should be? Are you prepared to go it alone? Because that is what might be the result of a hot-headed move. What if he is contrite, are you prepared to overlook even the most flagrant indiscretion? Or are you out for blood?

> *'How could he have left a receipt for condoms on his dresser? We have never used them.'*
>
> *'A brochure for a hotel and confirmation of a booking. What was that? For me it was the last bit of evidence I needed. I had to face him.'*

'I had no evidence to go on except my gut feelings. I just KNEW. And when I asked, I found out I was right.'

2

Why marriages break down

What counts in making a happy marriage is not so much how compatible you are, but how you deal with incompatibility.

(Leo Tolstoy)

Why do so many partnerships fail?

It is important to look at the reasons why so many families break up today. Understanding the causes, and being able to identify danger signals, will help you to monitor your own relationship if cracks occur.

In the present age people feel they have a right to individual happiness and fulfilment; they are not prepared to 'put up' with the kind of unsatisfactory relationships that so many of our grandparents tolerated. There is also the belief that the good life is there for us all to enjoy if we can only find it.

The whole approach to divorce has changed: it is now much more acceptable in society. No one is left out in the cold because they have been involved in a divorce. There is no scandal or shame attached to it any more. To be the 'other' woman or man is no longer a topic touched by shock or embarrassment. It is all too easy to believe that if others can manage this dance of changing partners and come out the other side, then so can you. What is often not so obvious is that deep-rooted feelings of guilt and remorse, even regret, stay around for a long time.

Magazines are full of advice about how to liven up your sex life, urging readers not to put up with less than 'perfect' sex. What does this mean? What suits one couple will not necessarily suit another, and it is foolish to try to rate your partner according to a scale of one to ten out of some magazine. And yet this is what a number of women and even some men do. They read the message as, 'If one partner won't do, seek out another.'

Does a long-term affair have the same impact on a relationship as a 'one-night-stand'? Both signal grave problems within the marriage. Both constitute a betrayal of a partner; even a fleeting sexual liaison may unravel the fabric of a relationship already under strain. The oft-heard phrase, 'It didn't mean a thing' sounds very different if you are the one listening to it being said by your partner.

A committed relationship should bring a sense of security, but for some the commitment works the other way and from the start some people find the constraint oppressive and feel imprisoned.

'On my wedding night I had a nightmare. In my sleep I took off my wedding ring and threw it across the room. Next morning we laughed, but I wonder now what my unconscious was telling me. Our marriage was on the rocks a year later.'

Danger ahead

This section will make you think carefully about how you felt in the early days of your relationship. If there are some things which dog your marriage, you will need to ask yourself, 'Have they been there from the beginning?'

However laid back we might like to think we are, we all have a picture in our minds of the kind of life we want for ourselves. From childhood we have dreams about our future, and although in those early years they may be about fame and fortune, we gradually adapt to something more realistic. How clear were you at the start about what your partner's dreams were for the future? How in tune was he with yours? Did you discuss your long-term desires? The picture *you* feel comfortable with as you try to peer into the years ahead, may be of yourself surrounded by children and grandchildren. Or, alternatively, you may hope for freedom and independence, and imagine yourself and your partner enjoying travel, changing jobs and even countries if the time feels right. Is this what your partner wants as well?

On another level, were you from the start prepared to accommodate your partner's interests if, for instance, he was into heavy-metal music or if he was a sports fanatic? Remember, something which mildly irritates you at the beginning of a relationship can really cause problems later. It just isn't fair to either of you to believe that your partner's passionate interest in golf or football will be abandoned once you are living together. If these topics haven't been discussed they can blow up later, and become a fertile ground for rows when you discover that these interests are indeed important to your partner, and not to be given up. If there is no room for negotiation and compromise, then trouble is fermenting.

Of course, you do not have to do everything together. You can each have separate interests. But, it helps to have the ability to slip into the other's shoes at times and to see the world through your partner's eyes. Your relationship will benefit from any understanding you bring to your partner's passionate interests.

> 'I really didn't understand why he had to go off cycling for hours. It was only when I swallowed hard and had a go myself, that I could begin to see the thrill of it. I will never go in for races, but I can understand why Josh loves to feel the freedom of it.'

Financial matters

Do you have the same views about what money should be spent on? There are more disagreements in a marriage about finance than almost anything else. One of the shocks which can come about when you first live together as a couple is to discover that you have different approaches to money. Arguments about whether to spend or to save may reflect conflicting values which extend far beyond money. If your idea of a good time is to plunge all your savings into an exotic holiday once a year, you are not going to be pleased when your husband feels that all extra cash should be ploughed into the home to make improvements. It may mean a lot to you to push the boat out when you celebrate birthdays or anniversaries, and if your partner believes this is a waste of money then you are heading for repeated rows and disappointment. Perhaps it goes against the grain and is inconceivable to you not to be lavish at times of celebration, but if your partner sees spending in this way as frivolous and unnecessary you are set on a collision course.

> 'I got a big promotion at work, so came home with a bottle of champagne. Tim's face fell when he saw what I had bought, and our celebration turned into our first fight.'

Decide in plenty of time before gifts have to be bought what your budget is. Family occasions like weddings or Christmas may bring to the fore disagreements about what you can or can't afford. Don't fall into the trap of concealing purchases which you know will, on discovery, infuriate your partner. That never works.

You may have opposite views too, on the subject of credit cards, overdrafts or even of managing debt. This is likely to have something to do with your parents' attitude to spending, and it is worth quite a bit of talking time together for you each to understand the other's feelings about funds and how to manage the family finances. Can you agree where the lines should be drawn? Can you agree on certain 'rules'? Are you the one who believes passionately about saving for a rainy day? If so, say so.

> *'I am not talking about going wild over spending, but I could see it actually hurt Billy if I bought something he felt we didn't really need. I decided to go back to work earlier than planned because then I felt freer to buy, and Billy didn't feel he was squeezed dry. The trouble came when we had a baby. I should have thought of that.'*

Sally had understood that Billy did have difficulties over money. Her sensitive use of the word 'hurt' shows that she could understand that Billy wasn't simply being awkward, but was genuinely troubled by too much obvious spending. So once they were settled in their new home, she went back to work to ease the burden on her husband. As she goes on to say, the problems arose when a child was born. This can be a flash point for any couple, as babies cost money, and a growing child even more. How do you decide what is a necessity for the baby or a luxury?

Another source of strain on any couple is where there is an earlier second family to consider, and a large slice of income has to go for maintenance or child support. If there has been a previous relationship this commitment will have to be taken into account right from the start. If there was cohabitation, the ex-partner will not be able to claim maintenance, but can still apply to the Child Support Agency for child support. On the other hand there may be a voluntary financial agreement, but either way, the second family will be affected by this call on family resources. This financial outlay can be a continual thorn in the side of a step or blended family. There may well be hidden costs too when a parent goes on visits to a child, and pays for entertainment or treats.

'We really had to count every penny. Yet money had to be found for Jim to travel to see his two children once a month. The cost really mounted. No one ever considers the stepfamilies.'

'I knew I had responsibilities for my ex-wife and daughter, yet I also knew it was very hard on my wife and kids. Every penny had to count. I certainly paid through the nose for my divorce, and went on paying.'

Planning ahead

You may have discovered already the wisdom of agreeing between you from the start about what is 'my money', 'your money' and 'our money'. Some couples can get along quite happily with the money being pooled in a joint account, but even so one or the other has to take overall responsibility for financial decisions. There is an old saying that the one who pays the first electricity bill pays it for the rest of a couple's life. So watch out!

If you want to plan for financial security on retirement and your partner sees that as premature or foolish, what will you do? Check out whether you are entitled to contribute to an occupational pension of your own. This is where there is wisdom in making sure that you have some money of your own to spend in the way you feel you want to. There is a mass of general, easy to understand, financial guidance to be seen on the Internet, so have a look around for information. Professional advice is never wasted, especially in the world of finance.

If one partner does not earn money it is still important for the 'family' money to be used jointly. If not, then finance can be used as a means of exerting control and this is never healthy in a relationship.

Tips for managing finance between you and your partner:

- Decide who will be responsible for each bill.
- Try to agree on a budget which covers gifts, celebrations, holidays, etc.
- Who will have the overall view of the family finances?
- Try to talk about the way *you* see the situation.
- Decide whether to have *our* money or *your* money and *my* money.
- Don't try to conceal purchases or expenditure.
- Don't let money become a source of power.
- If you are planning to have children, remember to think of the financial cost which will be involved.
- Don't forget to consider the expense of maintenance or child support commitments.
- Have you considered getting professional advice about financial planning?

Sexual compatibility

Are you sexually compatible? For someone to find themselves totally out of synch with a partner in this area will inevitably cause the sparks to fly. This isn't to say you both have to be ready and willing to make love at the drop of a hat. But you do need to get in tune with each other's timing, and this is the area where perhaps the most sensitivity is needed. Anyone with an underlying fear of intimacy may find closeness a problem, and in this case gentle understanding is much needed by the other partner. In the same way a partner with a higher sexual drive can experience very real anguish and distress if this divergence is not somehow resolved.

There are many ways of being sexual with each other, and affection and warmth during the day is a wonderful way of leading up to intercourse at night. Women too often complain that they are shown little tenderness, and expected to welcome their lover 'out of the blue'. A wise husband will have learnt that a cuddle or gentleness along the way will often lead to a very willing and sexual wife.

A compatible couple will also have learnt to read each other's signals and be able to respond to messages – sometimes invisible – indicating a need for closeness. A desire for intimacy can and does also spring from feelings of panic, anxiety, tension and a longing to be held and to feel safe. It is good to cling to each other physically in adversity just as it is good to celebrate your love and happiness for each other.

'He only ever touched me when he wanted sex. I would have liked a cuddle sometimes.'

'I never knew when it was the right time for her. She never gave me any signals. If I tried to get hold of her, she accused me of grabbing her.'

If you don't speak the same language of love, there will be misunderstandings and misinterpretations made along the way. What seems to be a mark of affection for one person, may seem to be overbearing for the other. This difference is often a contribution to the all-too-familiar scenario of a married man or woman finding sexual abandonment in an extra-marital affair.

'I often used to giggle to myself and think "if Norman could see me now" when I was in bed with Jock.'

'I found that I could do things to Annie I would never dream of doing with Grace.'

Both these couples had not been free enough to tell their partners what they wanted. Why? What inhibitions had prevented this happening? The answer is usually that they have kept a resentful silence, and waited for the other to guess at their fantasies. This is unfair.

Sharing

Do you share the same friends? Or if not, can you tolerate to some degree the mates your husband likes to bring home? Does your wife's gossiping with her women friends annoy you? Where do the in-laws fit in with your life together? Is there a bias towards his family or yours? Feelings about parents and in-laws need to be aired. Who keeps the family diary? Once again I ask you to think about whether you are sensitive enough to each other's needs?

Are you interested in each other's work? If there is an embargo on either one of you talking about worries at work, because it's 'boring' or 'too grim' or even 'too dreary for words' that denies the importance of what engages your partner during the day.

> *'Oh! he is something to do with tax, I think.'*
>
> *'Well, she is involved with marketing, whatever that means.'*

Detailed engineering projects or medical issues may not be your cup of tea, but if they are your partner's then each time you take an interest in what he tells you about them, you are strengthening the bonds between you. It is staggering to hear how little some men and women know about the nitty-gritty of the work their partner is engaged in. This suggests indifference to a partner, and opens the door for sharing interests with a colleague, with all that that can lead to.

Checklist for compatibility:

- Did you share dreams for the future together from the start?
- Were you happy about your future partner's outside interests?
- Did you agree, in general, on how money should be spent, and who should decide what?
- Did you feel you understood your partner's views about sex?
- Do you feel in tune, more or less, with your partner's family and friends?
- Are you interested in each other's work?
- Did you discuss when you would have children?

First check this list for compatibility as things stand today and then try to remember how it was when you first decided to be a couple. Think hard, and be fair.

Planning parenthood

There are several phases in a marriage which can usher in potential flash points. For many couples there is nothing quite so fraught as the period when the decision is being made about whether to start a family or not. It may come as a surprise to some happy couples to find they hold different views about the timing of a pregnancy, and about the whole question of childcare.

'I couldn't believe my ears when he said he had expected I would want to let his mother look after our baby so I could get back to work.'

'My mother was always at home for me. I couldn't agree to our baby being looked after by a stranger from a few weeks old. No way.'

There are, of course, couples who from day one are clear that they want children and proceed without much agonising; the only decision to be made is 'when'. But, even this is no longer as easy as it once was: some women today are high earners, so the financial implications may be great. If you are used to two incomes, then you need to have lengthy discussions about how you will manage: will the woman return to work sooner rather than later?

When your partner suddenly finds she wants to make the transition from being a couple into a family, it can make *you* suddenly become aware that it is a difficult and complex step to negotiate. This may be hard for her to understand if she has no worries about the changes ahead and sees a baby as a natural development of your loving relationship.

> *'She wanted to get pregnant. It was too soon for me, and I said so. Well, she did fall for a baby, and I didn't believe it was an accident. Things went from bad to worse.'*

Too many couples who eventually break up, do pinpoint the arrival of a baby as the beginning of the end of the marriage. I am not one of those people who think that conceiving a baby should be used to cement a marriage. Yet this happens all the time. Often a pact is made to have a child when there has been a rift: the baby is seen as the bond which will help the relationship under threat to hold fast. It is not unknown for someone who has strayed and then returned home, to agree to have a baby to convince his partner that he intends to stay.

But even the most stable couples must expect upheaval in their lives when they become parents. The arrival of a third person, a child, into the relationship brings about a shift in the family dynamics. In other words, it can affect the delicate balance of factors – both conscious and unconscious – which brought the couple together in the first place.

'I couldn't see why she wanted a baby now. We were so happy together.'

'I knew I would want a child one day. But my career had just taken off. How could he be so obtuse about what is important to me? Deciding on whether to get pregnant or not found us in the biggest disagreement we had ever had.'

Here again our own experiences in early family life can come to the fore. As strange as it may seem, if there was in-fighting between brothers or sisters which was not resolved when you were a child, then those painful feelings from long ago, of jealousy or fear of being replaced, may be felt again.

Anyone expecting his or her partner to provide continual mothering is setting out in a leaky vessel on the sea of matrimony, and the arrival of an infant can overturn the boat entirely. A man or a woman looking to his or her partner for parental affection and support will be at a loss to adjust to – move over and make room for – a baby.

Are you ready for parenthood:

- Do you feel your partner is as committed as you are to becoming a parent?
- Do you feel secure enough as a couple to make room for a baby?
- Is there any other reason which is influencing your decision to have a baby, like seeing a child as a way to 'mend a marriage'?
- Is this a good time to get pregnant? Consider finances, job prospects, housing conditions.

When baby makes three

A couple who are used to the freedom of being alone together may find it difficult to adjust to the restrictions which a pregnancy suddenly imposes. A wise couple will think in advance about this transformation which is going to change their lives, particularly as a difficult pregnancy can put a strain on even the strongest marriage.

The preparation for a baby's arrival is not just about buying the equipment babies now seem to need. There are decisions to be made on a variety of levels and happy are the couple who are in step about these. Indeed, this can be a joyous time as plans are made, names chosen, and time is available for dreaming about your baby. Once the baby arrives it is important that as a threesome you get to know each other. Many fathers now do not want, nor would they permit themselves, to be banished from the delivery room or nursery. Babies are no longer 'women's work' alone and the importance of the father in the lives of even very young babies is hopefully now fully acknowledged by both parents.

New parents run out of sleep – and sometimes patience – but if the underlying belief that 'we are now a family' is there, you will regroup into a family unit and delight in the fact that baby makes three. Sadly this is not always the case.

> *'I heard from my best friend that the night my son was born my husband took an old girlfriend out to supper. A year later I found out it was also the first time he was unfaithful to me.'*

A child with special needs

When a child is born with a disability this puts extra pressure on any family. Whereas some parents are able to pull together and take this as much in their stride as it is possible to do, there are some who find the strain of coping with a disabled child too much, and something breaks. Unfortunately, this may be the marriage, thus compounding an already difficult situation: any child takes time and energy, but a child who needs special care can drain the strength of even the most devoted parents.

If you are caring for a child with special needs you will have experienced your own private grief at the pain of it all. If you, as parents, can support each other, the family – especially if there are other children – will grow in strength. But, remember that there must be time for you to be together as a couple, otherwise you will not be able to maintain and 'top up' each other's strength. It may be very difficult to get away alone together, but arrangements must be made for occasional breaks if you are all to survive the long road ahead.

'She wouldn't leave him for a moment. Not a moment. After a bit it all got too much for me, and in the end I had to go. We had no life together any more.'

'He wouldn't accept there were many things our daughter wasn't able to do. He got impatient with us both. I don't believe he ever accepted how sick she was.'

'I always thought he was the kindest of men, but he never recovered from Jenny's birth. He said he couldn't take it, and never got involved with her. I was glad when he went.'

'It was as if she forgot we had two other children. She was with that baby twenty-four hours a day. It broke up our family.'

Share your feelings with each other about your attitude to having a disadvantaged child. Maybe your pride is hurt, maybe you feel somehow to blame, maybe you are deeply angry that this has happened to your family, and maybe your partner has similar feelings. If these are not expressed, and shared, they will be stored up and will eventually find an outlet which is both disruptive and hurtful.

> **Acting together to cope with a child with special needs:**
>
> - Share the sadness of the situation with your partner.
> - Get all the help you can.
> - Don't fall into the trap of thinking you are the only one who can look after your child.
> - Don't blame yourself, your partner, or your child for what has happened.
> - Involve family, friends, support agencies, social services.

Childlessness

Sadly, deciding to have a baby does not always go according to plan. What if you and your partner are 'ready', but there is no sign of a pregnancy? This puts an almost unbearable pressure on most couples. Even those who at the start are philosophical and believe that babies come in their own time, often begin to despair as the months or years go by. For the woman especially, there is a visible reminder each month that conception has not taken place. Indeed, as a woman becomes even more in tune with her body, carefully plotting days of ovulation, bitter disappointment occurs with unfailing regularity.

You may have already found, too, that you are not spared embarrassing pressure from well-meaning friends and family who ask the most intimate questions. You may even be on the receiving end of accusations of 'selfishness' or half-joking instructions to 'get on with it'.

> *'I could only face people and try and smile while saying "We're trying". That at any rate brought an embarrassed laugh.'*
>
> *'I had to stop going to my in-laws. They kept asking me when I was going to make them grandparents.'*

What begins as a slight annoyance can quickly become a major anxiety. The months pass, and this is where the strain can build up in even the most loving relationships. It may, quite unreasonably, stir up doubts and worries about your own or your partner's sexuality and even sexual identity. And when does the nagging question, 'Is it *my* fault or *my partner's*?' creep in? Although this thought might be banished as soon as it surfaces, it will return. Either, or both of you, may be reluctant to seek a medical opinion, and this too can be a source of disagreement. Being hesitant to seek professional help stems from fear of what you may hear.

> 'He wouldn't come to the doctor's with me or even really talk about it. I wanted a baby so badly. That was the beginning of the end for us.'
>
> 'We had all the tests, and then it was worse. We were told to go away as they couldn't understand why she didn't conceive.'

Today, with fertility treatment so widely known and spoken about, it is as well to seek some medical advice sooner rather than later. But, as you may know from experience, this procedure is in itself a strain on the strongest couple. There can be many disappointments on the way. Lovemaking which was so joyful can suddenly be constrained by calendars and temperature graphs. From listening to men and women in this situation, I have found it is the men who often find the outside interventions the most difficult to deal with. The women seem to suffer with the grief of the 'failure' of it all, since, unfortunately, that is often what it feels like: failure. The strain of the situation can lead to the couple breaking up as they struggle to make decisions about when is the 'right' time to have sex, whether to continue with IVF treatment, or whether to plan their life together without a child.

If conception does not take place for any reason, there are some couples who are able to say to each other, 'It just wasn't meant to be' and really believe this. Others find it impossible to deal with it in that way, and a rift grows wider as the months, and years, pass by. If this is your battle, would you consider seeing a counsellor? It could be that you are holding mistaken beliefs which add to your burden. For example, you may have convinced yourself that if there is no baby your partner will leave you in time, and it is surprising how potent these self-fulfilling prophecies can be. You may feel that *you* are being blamed, and being seen as a disappointment. In fact, your partner may not actually be so bothered and it is important that these thoughts and feelings are aired and shared, especially when there is such an emotionally charged issue at large.

A similar situation can occur after a miscarriage. It is tragic to hear that this loss often divides a couple. A miscarriage is a bereavement and if a couple react to this in different ways the relationship may never be repaired. Talk, talk and talk about what you are feeling. Whether there is no baby at all, or whether you have had a miscarriage, you will feel bereaved and as a couple you need to go through this together.

'I had a miscarriage. Kevin just seemed to go on with everyday life, while I was very depressed. A year later we broke up. Would we have anyway? I just don't know, but I don't think so.'

'I didn't give her the support I should have done at the time. We began to drift apart, and it was then I met Martha. It was the miscarriage alright that did it. I didn't know then what I know now and I am sorry about that.'

'Sometimes I wanted to leave the whole thing for a bit, yet Anne wouldn't let a month go by without trying.'

'We had all the tests and nothing was wrong. That's when we both began to blame each other.'

'He had a child before, so I felt dreadful that I couldn't conceive. I lost all confidence in myself and got very depressed. Everyone else seemed to be pregnant.'

'Our relationship definitely began to fall apart. I thought at the time it was because we couldn't have a child. Now I am not so sure, and perhaps in view of what happened it is as well I didn't get pregnant. When I married a year later, we started a baby right away. No problems.'

Childlessness: pay special attention to these points:

- If conception does not take place make sure you understand exactly how your partner feels.
- Tell your partner how *you* are feeling.
- Decide *together* what steps you want to take.
- Beware of blaming the other – it could be because you are afraid that it is 'your' fault.

It can be fraught with danger, too, for a couple who have previously agreed not to have children, if one of them has a change of heart. A promise and agreement made early on in the relationship takes on a very different hue. This is a very important consideration which must be faced full on. Have you, or your partner, changed your stance on this issue? If so, why is this? Is it because you have been under pressure from family or friends to get pregnant, and been told you are 'selfish' if you do not become a parent? Or is it something you feel inside yourself and you now really desire to become a mother or father?

'He got me to agree we wouldn't have children. Ten years on we broke up and he remarried. Nine months later he had a child.'

The silver wedding divorce

Did you know that there are now many more divorces in the older age group, among 'seniors'? The dream of unruffled serenity for our 'golden years' is no longer guaranteed. Better health, better opportunities for women, and living longer have all contributed to this changed attitude.

Now that the ignominy of divorce has been eroded, men and women who have been together for almost a lifetime feel free to make a cruel move which would have been virtually unheard of a few years back. It may surprise you to know that people in their fifties, sixties and even seventies are not immune to the changing sexual patterns of today. It can come as a tremendous shock to 'adult' children to find that Mum and Dad are breaking up and definitely *not* feeling over the hill. Almost invariably this is a completely one-sided decision, and the partner left behind finds recovery immeasurably harder than someone in their thirties or forties. At the time when so many friends are coping with the death of a spouse, there is something very different about being left by a partner of many years' standing.

> *'Can you believe he went after fifty years of marriage? I have nothing now. All my life was spent looking after him and the children. I am quite alone.'*
>
> *'How could he leave me now? I am seventy-four. I could have managed when I was fifty, now I am old and alone.'*

Eileen had decided years ago *not* to confront her husband each time she knew he was involved with someone else. She waited for it to blow over, and felt that the security of family life would be enough to restrain her husband; it was something he would never risk losing. The blow when it came was thus doubly cruel, and Eileen was left with the deep resentment of not having brought things to a head years earlier.

And it isn't always the grieving woman who is left behind. Work options and a chance to travel may prompt even the most staid wife to believe that life must be lived to the full before it is too late.

> *'I wasn't ready to give up on life. All he wanted when he retired was to sit by the telly; I wanted to see the world, and found a good man to go with me. I had to take the chance. I don't think I was missed.'*

3

Must there be a divorce?

This is what divorce is: taking things you no longer
want from people you no longer love.
(Zadie Smith, *White Teeth*)

What if we stay together?

Marriages can, and do, get mended. BUT, and this is a very important 'but', both of the partners have to want this to happen. It is a grave error to think that just because your relationship has become stressful, there is only one way to go, and that it must be the downward slope to splitting up. So what will it be like if you pull back from the brink? Put the brake on for a moment, and see if you can reverse the Humpty-Dumpty process of a threatened divorce. It will be hard, but it can be done.

Ask yourself what it will be like if you stay together. Are you prepared for some changes? It may be uncomfortable to think about whether you have contributed to the crisis, but be honest with yourself. If you don't understand why this relationship has reached a crossroads you will run the risk of repeating the same situation again in the future. If you are able to take at least a small proportion of the blame this can lead to a feeling of inner strength and a mark of goodwill that you intend to make a go of it.

Have you been flexible? Perhaps that is what you are trying to be now, and looking to see if there are still options open to you both. Or have you been stuck in the groove of knowing your relationship was unhappy, but just fearing it could only get worse. Can you pull yourself out of that way of thinking?

Can you find a way to prevent your feelings building up to such a pitch that they burst out from one or other of you? If in the past you yourself have started destructive arguments instead of constructive discussions, can you change that? If you can both find a way of holding out a hand to each other there is every possibility that you can go on. However, make quite sure that neither of you assumes the role of martyr and says 'I can forgive, but never forget'. Of course, if your partner has betrayed you the pain will, to some extent, stay with you whatever happens. But no healthy relationship can survive if one of you moves into a position of power for the reasons that the 'other' has broken their vows of fidelity or caused a crisis in some other way. So make sure that does not happen. No marriage can be repaired or retrieved if these feelings are in the air.

Were you out of touch?

Were you like Linda – mentioned before – who had been unhappy for so long. Why had she been unable to decode her own feelings and to admit that something was very wrong? Does it sound familiar to you to be so afraid of rocking the boat by being straight with your partner that you don't talk about your unhappiness? By not being true to herself, Linda had made the situation more grave.

> 'For months I kept quiet. I didn't know how to fuss really.'

Men are not immune from this way of hiding their head in the sand either. George – also mentioned earlier – must have been very much out of touch with his wife to be so unaware of the gap between them and the mess the relationship was in. Ask yourself what he gained by allowing himself to be blind to it all? Indeed, his wife may have thought his silence was indifference. So learn from Linda and George, and vow you will never let up on continuing to be involved and intimate with your partner.

Why you chose your partner in the first place

Take a moment to take stock. Why did you marry your partner? What attracted you to him in the first place? You may be surprised to find your answer reveals that what first attracted you is the cause of what annoys you most now: a man or woman with high sexual drive and sex-appeal may have seemed a prize to be won at the time. But later experience may show you have paid a high price if you have to fight off others attracted in the way you were!

'I came from a family which always argued. I found it bliss to be with a man who always gave way to me. Ten years on his indecision drives me mad.'

'When I was a kid we were very poor and always in debt. The girlfriend I lived with was very careful with money and I liked that. Now I just see her as mean.'

A boyfriend with a laid-back attitude may seem appealing, but a partner who will never give an opinion about anything will be frustrating, at the very least, to live with for the rest of your life.

Some people still like to believe that marriages are made in heaven. In fact, they are on their way to being made when we are babies, since it is from the people around us in our earliest years that we learn to love and to be loved. Children keep an eye on their parents' relationship. They watch how they treat each other, how they work out conflicts, and – on an unconscious level – absorb all this into their view of how adults get along together. It is as important for kids to see parents discussing major issues, and at times disagreeing, as it is for them to see parents enjoying each other's company and laughing together.

Anyone not loved, really loved, as a baby will find it difficult to believe that someone can ever love them. When a person comes along who wants to be with them and says so, the attraction of this alone may bring about such a surge of relief – 'Someone loves me after all' – that they make a hasty and unsatisfactory match. Mere availability is no real basis for a lasting relationship.

At times the unconscious search for a parent we never had contributes to our choice of a mate. Being 'mothered' or 'fathered' as an adult may in the early days together have some appeal, but as we mature our needs change. It is then that a marriage based on such factors can become claustrophobic and make one of the partners look for a way out. Also, fear of being left on the shelf, and without a partner when the music stops, can propel someone into a marriage. The old saying 'marry in haste, repent at leisure', is never more apt than when a couple marry for these reasons, and not because of genuine love and commitment.

Fortunately women have, in the main, been released from the urgency of finding a husband in order to escape from the parental home and from the shame of being unmarried. However, not all women have financial independence, and there are still too many early commitments made so as to flee from an emotionally or physically abusive home. I hope this does not sound familiar to you.

One of the ingredients for a happy marriage is when both partners have developed enough of their own identities to be able to merge into a couple while at the same time not losing site of who they are. If a union is formed *before* this growing-up period has taken place, then the danger is that one will grow at a different pace and the other will be left behind. At a recent wedding I attended I heard the bride and groom vow to 'give each other room to grow'. This made my heart glow.

> *'It was okay to be babes-in-the-wood together in our twenties. It began to pall in our thirties.'*

The tangle of an unhappy marriage is often centred around issues of independence or dependence. Fortunate are the couples who can be flexible, and who can move easily from showing vulnerability on occasions to strength at other times.

> *'I had a hopeless dad, so when I met my husband he made me feel very safe, but after a couple of years I found him authoritarian and just plain bossy.'*

Many men and women want to escape from marriages which have hit the doldrums. But just changing partners, however attractive this proposition may be, is no guarantee that 'second time around' will be an easier ride. The statistics for the number of second marriages which fail bear testimony to this. And remember, the number of second marriages which come to grief is even higher if there are children from an earlier relationship.

Whether it is you or your partner who decides that it is time to go your separate ways, be prepared for the grief which will surely follow. However tempestuous a relationship has become, there was almost certainly love for each other at the start. Many men and women who can't wait to leave an old loved one behind, find to their shock that it is not at all easy to do.

> *'I wasn't prepared for the blind panic I felt when we decided to split up.'*

Can a marriage be rekindled?

What kind of a marriage did you have before you felt things went so wrong? Would you like to get back to that time? If you think about it, you may surprise yourself by saying, 'It wasn't so good then, either'. So what do you want? Of course there are couples who weather the most terrible marital storms, and even seem to thrive on them. Only think of Elizabeth Taylor and Richard Burton whose marriage, divorce and remarriage made such headlines. Think of the late Alan Clark, a well-known womanizer, who was nevertheless greatly loved by his wife Jane. 'Anyway,' she says, 'if you know you're loved, it's fine'. Not many women would agree with her, but some do.

No marriage can go back to how it was, and it would be foolish to think otherwise. You will find it was easier to fall in love the first time around. A second go means you not only need good intentions, but you must have a determination as well. Nevertheless, you may, with a lot of talking, decide that there is too much at stake to throw it all away. Your time together with all those shared memories counts for too much and a new formula can be worked out. This route calls upon complete honesty from both of you about what you want for the future.

Have you considered finding a professional to talk to? It may be the moment when you need outside advice and should talk things over with a trained marital counsellor. It is often easier to discuss things, however painful, with a sympathetic and trained person rather than with someone you know.

What do you think makes a happy marriage:

Ask yourself these questions about your contribution to the relationship. Be honest!

- Did you have expectations from the beginning of what you both would contribute to the marriage?

- Do you think you have kept your part of the bargain? (Remember, this is tell-the-truth time.)
- Are you trying to recreate the relationship you saw between your parents?
- Are you attempting to create an entirely different scenario to the family you were brought up in?
- Do you have a blueprint about how a marriage 'should' be?
- Do you think that in a marriage a couple should never have any disagreements?
- Do you believe that marriage should be like the best of your courtship days?
- Do you think you and your partner should almost magically know what the other is thinking?
- Do you believe that being married should solve all your problems, including being lonely?

Look at your answers, consider them carefully. What do they tell you about your view of marriage? Do your answers pass the reality test? Perhaps you answered 'maybe' to some of the questions. But, think hard about what message you are giving to yourself. Did you find yourself with a wry smile on your face when you remembered that you did think love would be enough to see you through? Perhaps that smile vanished when you asked yourself if you had lived up to the bargain, and to the promises you made when you became a couple.

Was there a 'yes' or a 'no' to the question about marriage being like your courting days? If you answered in the affirmative you need to go on to think about this. This is what I meant when I asked if your answers passed the reality test. The trick about making love last through the years is not to sigh over the good old days and keep comparing them to today. By all means keep a special place in your memories, and your heart, for those golden days when you first began to spend time together and realized that he or she might be 'the one'. But nothing stays the same. Think how dull it would be if that were so. Indeed it is important that we do keep a hold of those images, and nothing can be sweeter than from time to time to be drenched in nostalgia and to share those reminiscences. But life goes on, and we all need to continue building on our store of happy days. Just think how much fun it used to be to stay awake until the small hours talking about how to change the world. However, with an early start for work, or to be up with the children, it may mean you count the precious hours of sleep. But that doesn't rule out an equally memorable evening spent at home together in front of the fire. In fact, as our lives seem to get busier and busier it is important to make sure that as a couple you find time just to be together. And that *is* like the 'good old days' when you couldn't wait to be by yourselves. Remember?

Have you surprised yourself by some of your answers? *Did* you think that being married would mean you had a guarantee to live happily ever after? That you would never again be lonesome or feel afraid? What do you think about that assumption now? How realistic was it and was it based on the fairy tales of our story books or on Hollywood? Consider whether you can accept a more adult version of those accounts. One where a couple can accept that there are faults both within themselves and their partner. With love comes generosity, and if we can be tolerant of our lover (and of ourselves) it makes for a much more comfortable and loving relationship.

Ways to save a marriage

Have you decided to try to save your marriage at all costs? Even though you want to give it up or your partner has said he wants to go, there may be a moment when you both decide to have one more try. If this is so, think carefully about how you view each other. What does your partner see reflected back when he looks into your eyes? Is there anger, dismissal, mistrust, or boredom? What do *you* see when you look into your partner's eyes? Have you considered this? Are you both *really* willing to take those essential steps towards each other to bridge the rift which has appeared? Do you believe that you have a chance of turning things around – or are you just going through the motions? Be honest. Stop and think very carefully.

There will be things you will both have to change. Are you prepared for this? If you have both focussed on outside interests as a way of avoiding each other's company, are you prepared to give them up? Getting together may well mean you both have to make sacrifices to regain that sense of being a couple.

If you feel trapped in a cycle of conflict, how do you plan to escape from this? The way you speak to your partner (even the tone of voice you use) will either begin to smooth over the rift or add fuel to the fire. You will find your behaviour towards your partner will influence his attitude to you. If you are still locked in battle and feel you are justified in 'having a go' from time to time, then most likely you will also be on the receiving end of enemy fire. Are you willing to keep a check on yourself and not always point out every fault in your partner? Of course there will be times when he treads on your toes, or says or does something which you feel is insensitive. But at this very fragile time in your relationship it is not always in your best interest to make an issue out of every single thing. Are you ready to pause and then decide when to speak up and when it is wise to bite your tongue? What is most important to you – to be together again, or to point out you are right every time?

Too many people misread the signals which come from their own emotions. Are you waking early in the morning feeling distressed with fear and apprehension? We usually assume this springs from anxiety whereas it could be masking rage and aggression. Try to understand what is going on inside yourself, because if *you* don't know, how can you expect your partner to, and how will he be able to act in a way to make you feel better? If romance has gone out of the window and you are trying with a feet-on-the-ground attitude to mend your relationship, find time to care for each other and to get back into the habit of anticipating your lover's needs. It may be hard to re-start a sexual relationship if the spectre of 'somebody else' is still in your thoughts.

Use this checklist to see if you have a chance of making a go of it:

- Can you say 'I love you' and still mean it?
- Can you reinstate that 'good morning' and 'good night' kiss?
- Can you still appreciate your partner, and say so?
- Can you seriously consider compromises you can both make?
- Can you find a way of spending more time together?
- Can you balance romance and reality?
- Are you prepared to seek professional help?
- Can you truly agree to work together to make a fresh start?
- Are you prepared to give the relationship time to heal?
- Can you feel optimistic about the future and your relationship?
- Can you think of ways to cherish your partner?
- Can you think of ways to help rekindle your passion for each other?
- Are you ready to take on more than your share of responsibility to make it work?
- Are you prepared to accept at least some of the blame for what has happened?
- Can you keep alive the memories of the good times you shared in the past?
- Can you find the enthusiasm to get back in touch with your partner, physically and emotionally?
- Is 'sorry' a word you can say?

If there are more 'yes's than 'no's, then have a go.

The first 'rule' is to give yourselves time. Take things slowly, and don't expect miracles. If you or your partner has been unfaithful, then how you behave in bed together will be a sensitive issue to start with. Remember, intercourse is not the only way to show each other you care. You will need to display generosity and kindness, and it may have been some time since you shared these sentiments.

You may be shocked to remember just how long! You may even find you need to cry together. No harm in that. In fact, tears can help the healing process, especially after such a painful time. Whether you are the one who wanted to leave, or the one left behind, both of you will have felt the distress of a troubled relationship. You will both be counting the emotional cost and trying to recover from a wound, even if it is only to your pride.

> 'Say sorry? Me? I have nothing to be sorry about. I wasn't the one who had a fling. But hang on, I am sorry that this has happened to us and I could say that I suppose.'

Should you stay together for the sake of the children?

If you decide to stay together 'for the kids' sake' make sure that this really is the reason, and that you both believe in it with all your heart. Also, make sure that you have both resolved not to tell the children that this was the reason. Possession of this knowledge will place a very heavy burden on them, especially if they are still witnesses to an unhappy relationship which isn't working out. Don't let the excuse of staying together for the children's sake mask your own fear of leaving home, nor let it be used to blackmail your partner into staying against his will. If this is used as a weapon, rather than something you both genuinely feel, it can only succeed in wounding everyone. Nothing can destroy family life quite so swiftly as resentment and spite. And once these emotions take seed they rapidly grow until they engulf the whole family.

> 'He told the kids he would not be leaving. Guess what? Six months later he left to live with her. The kids were devastated. Holly kept asking me "What did I do?"'

> *'He said he would stay and give her up. It was a bad decision because although we tried he left a year later.'*

The truth is that there is no right, or best, time to leave children. Although there are many ways that they can be helped, children always suffer during and after their parents' break-up. (See Chapter Five). The finding of Judith Wallenstein, who is considered to be the world's expert on the effects of divorce on children, is that the major impact of divorce is felt when the 'children' become adult and they choose their own partners. In her latest book, *The Unexpected Legacy of Divorce*, she devotes a lot of space to 'the voices which belong to the children of divorce now grown to adulthood'. Those 'voices' are, alas, full of anguish and very painful to listen to.

> *'Gary and I were on the brink of a divorce, but then agreed we could and should do something to sort out our relationship, because we did agree that at the root of all our troubles, we were good parents.'*

The most important principle to hold onto, whether you are leaving or being left or are in an unhappy marriage, is that throughout the upheaval you must both remember you are still parents. Children must be protected from learning all the details and although it may be hard to accept, whatever has happened between you both, to your children you are still their mum and dad. The greatest disservice you can do for your children is to try to get them on your side by describing to them every fault of your partner; for in that case you will be verbally attacking their father or mother.

If you are going to separate then you need to start to be, at the very least, polite to your soon-to-be ex, because you are setting in motion rules of behaviour for the future. Although at the moment it may be hard to think beyond the next few weeks or months, remember you are going to be parents for a long time to come. So everything is to be gained by being able to agree that you will continue to do your best to cooperate with each other over parenting. There will be family occasions over the years and so if you can manage the day-to-day issues now, it will be easier later to accommodate bar or bat mitzvahs, graduations, weddings and one day in the future, the birth of grandchildren.

Too late for talking?

What if too much has happened even to think of trying again to mend the rift? Perhaps you have, over the years, tried every way you can think of to build bridges with your partner, only to have them blown up each time by another bout of drinking or another 'fling'. You may also have grown tired of listening to excuse after excuse.

> 'Man wasn't meant to be monogamous. Okay, I did stray, but she always seemed to understand. Then one day I came home and she'd gone. I couldn't believe it. Why now?'
>
> 'Each time we "had a talk" he would promise me the earth. What was the point of one more all-night discussion?'

How do you know when it is time to call it a day and to decide that enough is enough? Gillian told me it was the saddest day of her life when she packed her case and left. She said that Hugh had always been able to talk her out of leaving, but this time the discovery of one more infidelity made her determined to make the break. 'Quite honestly, I was all talked out.'

> 'I suddenly knew, just knew, I had done all I possibly could to save our marriage. It was time to call it a day.'

So, how do you leave your partner?

According to the song there are 'fifty ways to leave your lover', but it is surprisingly difficult actually to do so. Do you leave a note? Surely your ex deserves more than a 'Dear John' letter, and yet there are not many couples who can shake hands and wish each other well. Some couples decide to seek professional help in order to part on better terms and to find a way of untangling their feelings for each other.

If there have been considerable difficulties in the relationship for a while then the idea of breaking up may just fly out in anger from one of you. It may have been somewhere at the back of your mind that this is where you are heading, but it still comes as a shock when you hear yourself, or your partner, actually saying the words. But what if there has been no prior discussion and your partner is unaware of the growing rift between you, while you may have already begun to contemplate and to accept it? You will probably have given a lot of thought to whether you are going to leave, and this alone will have helped, to some degree, to prepare you for the actual parting of the ways. If you have a new lover, you will have spent hours discussing your future together and even talked about the expected fall-out from present partners.

But, although the actual parting may seem comparatively straightforward in theory, in practice it will be much more difficult than you could possibly have imagined. You may have come to the brink of telling your partner that you are leaving many times before you actually come out with it. The pressure is enormous as you try to find a way to break the news, especially if you have a new love waiting in the wings who cannot understand what the delay is about.

'The way we were' – the words of this popular song have brought tears to the eyes of many who thought they could not be touched by such sentimentality. But there it is, and the sentiment accounts for the difficulty that arises when someone vows to leave their wife or husband but then discovers reasons why it can't be *now*.

If you are the 'other' man or woman beware of trying to speed up the process in your favour by direct action, since this may spring from a sense of frustration and anger rather than love and appreciation of your lover's dilemma. It may also misfire!

> *'In the end I picked up the phone and rang his wife. Of course, then he had to leave her, but it wasn't in a way I would have liked.'*
>
> *'I want to know how I can help my lover leave his wife. I know he loves me, yet keeps dithering. What can I do?'*
>
> *'I came home fired up to tell her I was going. She opened the door looking so sweet with that lovely smile, and I just couldn't do it. It took another two years before I was able to tell her. I think it was just as cruel in the end.'*

If your partner is unsuspecting about what is about to crash into their life, you must be ready for fireworks. Prepare yourself for your partner's complete and utter devastation! Even if things have been pretty rocky for some time there is a big difference between continued negotiation and a total break-up. In this situation there is no easy phrase which is the equivalent of 'I love you' or 'I want us to be together for the rest of our lives' which can trip off your tongue with ease. You may know the latest love songs, but these don't provide the catch phrases to say to someone we once loved, 'I have to tell you I now love someone else' or 'I want a divorce!' The one who throws the bombshell will also experience piercing pain, but not as much as the one to whom the blow is being dealt.

> *'It nearly killed me trying to find a way to tell her I was leaving. I lost three stone, looked haggard and found it difficult to believe anyone at all could love me, let alone two wonderful women.'*

> '*I was having a love affair and I wanted a divorce and decided to tell my husband. I gave myself a deadline of Sunday evening. I reckoned on his being SO angry he'd tell me to clear off. I couldn't have been more wrong. He cried and begged me to stay.*'

Rosemary had hoped, perhaps unconsciously, that her husband's anger would help her to go. She banked on his furious reaction to aid her to slice their relationship in two. She told me she had rehearsed the scene in her mind over and over again and imagined the most awful row, with her packing and storming out of the flat. In fact she ended up crying too, and comforting Stan and promising to stay. Rosemary and Stan split up three months later. Quite possibly they needed that time to effect the parting, which was something Rosemary had not bargained on.

So what does it take to have the courage to face your partner and say, 'Sorry, but I'm off' or 'I can't stay in this relationship any more'. You may feel that 'courage' isn't the right word and that 'cowardice' is more appropriate. The reality is that if these words are to be said, it does need a lot of pluck, and a degree of ruthlessness, actually to say them. To my way of thinking it takes guts to sever a relationship in this way, and the real coward is the one who e-mails or faxes the news to a partner that a relationship is over. Believe me, these things do happen. If you find you just cannot say the words, this could be a strong indication that there is part of you which does not *want* to say them, and you will not be the first, or the last, lover to pull back at the last moment. Not being able to utter these words when it comes to the moment of truth can lead to the creation of 'double families'. This is when a 'husband', who is quite likely a father, is shared between two women who may or may not know about the other's existence. Not at all an easy situation to manipulate.

Is the solution for you just to disappear? I cannot think of a worse thing to do to another human being, unless – and only unless – you are in fear of your life. Where the relationship has been overshadowed by violence this may be the wise thing to do, at least for a while. Another solution would be for you to have someone with you when you tell your partner you are leaving. Someone who will be there to protect you if you have a pretty good idea that your partner will attack you upon hearing the news. If there is any likelihood of this happening you should also make sure in advance that you have somewhere to go.

Behind the emotional abuse, the beatings and the fear experienced by some women and men there is also the worry that the out-of-control partner may hurt the children. If there is a possibility of this happening, make sure they are out of the way when you break the news. There is increasing awareness of domestic violence: this is a term which covers emotional, psychological and physical abuse. I wonder if you know that domestic violence forms the second most common type of violence reported to the police in Britain. So, if abuse of this kind is familiar to you, it is advisable to seek professional support before taking any action. Domestic violence is not a problem which only applies to 'other' people, as perhaps you know only too well. It affects men, women and children on a frightening scale. Money, race or class play no part in this. I say more about domestic violence in Chapter Six.

If the cards have been on the table for some time and the end of your relationship is accepted by you both, it may be possible to decide together that one or the other of you will move out at an agreed date.

> 'We agreed I would move out when he was away on a business trip. I couldn't have gone through all that "Is this yours or mine?" rubbish.'

If there are children to consider, then this will have a colossal impact on them and so who leaves the home, when and where, will be a tremendous issue.

> **If you have resolved to leave your partner:**
>
> - There is no easy way to tell your partner you are leaving. Be prepared for this.
> - However tempting it might be to duck out of a face-to-face meeting, consider whether or not your partner deserves the additional pain of receiving the news by letter, fax or telephone call.
> - Remember, there is no way you can predict your partner's reaction to the bombshell you are going to drop.
> - Are you prepared to say you are involved with someone else, if that is the case, and who that person is?
> - Are you prepared to answer intimate questions about your affair: 'Is she better in bed than I am?'
> - Can you bear to be challenged with the lies and deception which has enabled you to have an affair? ('Oh my God, you never did go to your college reunion, did you?')

Have you already separated?

Has the door already slammed shut? If this has happened then the first step must be for you to care for yourself. Even if you have young children you must find time to protect your own physical and emotional health. Safeguarding your family must start with yourself. It is a grave error to think you can manage on your own; this is the time to call on friends and family to give all the support they can. A friend arriving with a prepared meal to share after the children are in bed can be a life-saver. Remember, though, that friends will have made up their minds about your partner mostly from what you have told them. If, in the past, you have confided some of the hurtful details, don't be surprised if they are less than sympathetic and tell you that you are better off. This may not be what you want to hear. And they may find your mixed feelings hard to understand. Speaking to a counsellor is often a wise thing to do as well, since even the closest friends and family do not always have the professional experience to guide you in the best way.

In the midst of all the confusion and hurt, it is important to begin to think of the practical issues too. If you feel that this is just too much to consider, then perhaps you have a friend or relative who can help you to sort out the hundred and one things which will need to be dealt with.

Remember that you will be particularly vulnerable at this time, and you may think that an extra alcoholic drink will take the edge off the pain of separation. One drink will probably be alright, but take heed. That first drink can soon become two, or three, or more. Indeed, kind and well-meaning friends may suggest drowning your sorrows as a remedy for your grief, so beware. Take care, too, that drugs (either prescribed, or not) don't become a way of temporarily blunting the hurt. You will only be storing up trouble for the future. In fact this is a time when it is important for you to be particularly clear-headed.

> 'I stopped having even a glass of wine. I knew once I began drinking I wouldn't be able to stop.'

You may find that your eating habits change dramatically. If you have been used to cooking a meal every evening, or having one cooked for you, the temptation might be to say, 'I can't bother by myself'. Indeed, eating alone may be one of the hardest things to do at first.

> 'We always enjoyed our dinner together. We made a point of eating well, and talking over the day. Now I can't face the loneliness, it seems so sad to eat alone.'

If this is a problem for you, try to find a friend or colleague to share a meal with. Even if you find you have no appetite because of the pain and churning in your stomach, it is surprising how some food can slip down if you are chatting to a mate. Don't go to the other extreme and buy yourself food which will make you put on pounds! Of course, if you are having trouble eating, you are 'allowed' to tempt yourself with food you like best. But know when to draw the line. Putting on a lot of weight will not help you to feel good about yourself.

Try to resist the temptation to burn the candle at both ends. You may feel you want to show your ex that you are desirable and have a very active social life. If you are the one who has been left behind this is understandable, but remember that you must have time to absorb all that has been happening as well as to begin to plan your future.

Watch out for someone of the opposite sex who moves in on you too soon. Your vulnerability may be obvious and if your self-image is low you may mistake someone's interest in you for love, when it may be lust. If you are feeling sexually bereft this may be very appealing, but do watch out, as six months down the line you may have wished you had waited until you could make a more careful and informed choice of a new partner.

First aid. How to help yourself:

- **Get support** This is the time to call on friends and family. If there is truly no one to turn to, find a counsellor, because you must talk to someone about the situation.
- **Get organized** Make a list of your assets and your partner's. Look at what joint financial responsibilities you have. i.e. mortgage, joint bank account, pension rights, wills etc
- **Don't try to blur the pain with drugs or alcohol** It is all too easy to start on pills to make you sleep, pills to take the edge off the pain, or that extra glass of wine.
- **Build up a network** Although couples may still make you welcome, it can be hard at first to be the only one on your own. Seek out other singles. There are plenty around. Can you find a way of spending more time with them?

- **Make sure you eat** The trap is to stop cooking. Don't get caught into thinking, 'What's the point of cooking for one?' Okay, so buy some comfort food, but don't go overboard.
- **Get rest** The temptation can be to race around to show the world you are still alive and very active. This is especially so if you are the one who has been left. But you need time to digest what is happening and to plan for your future.
- **Don't rush into a new relationship** The temptation is to show the world (and your ex) that you are desirable and someone loves you. It can give your confidence an immediate boost, but you may be getting involved for all the wrong reasons.

Part Two

Going Through a Divorce

If you are going through hell, keep going.
(Winston Churchill)

4

What a divorce really means

The world I deal with is full of cruel stories.
(Noël Coward, *The Astonished Heart*)

So, what does divorce entail?

A divorce means more, much more, than obtaining a piece of paper which says your marriage is over. So prepare yourself for all that is to come. If you have decided, or had it decided for you, that this is the only way to go, then brace yourself for the next set of hurdles. There will be practical things to deal with and a number of other more major issues, which you may not have expected. They will all have to be negotiated, one way or another. Keep in mind that if you have found your partner disagreeable and difficult to deal with during marriage, the difficulties are likely to increase tenfold when you start discussing how to untangle your life together.

Saying goodbye

For some couples, saying 'goodbye' can be synonymous with saying 'good-riddance'. However, that may not be what *you* really feel or *want* to feel, so it may take years before you and your partner can say goodbye and truly wish that the other has a happy life.

> *'I loved her and would like to have found a way to stay together, but she said goodbye, and went. I find it very hard to wish her well, but I pray one day I will be able to. I still love her, you see.'*

If you are parents, then the divorce will put additional pressure on you both as you have to negotiate arrangements about the children together. It may also mean that you are forced by circumstances to go on seeing each other quite frequently when handing over the children. As hard as it may be to accept this now, it might go on for years. This contact can, of course, prolong the feelings of distress, especially grief, if you are still in love with your ex. Friends and family may find it hard to understand that against all the odds you still love your partner very much indeed. Saying goodbye to the life you had together may be torture for you every step of the way. So hearing those you love tell you that you are better off without him, or to 'get a new life' will make you feel the knife is being twisted in the wound.

> *'I liked being married. I didn't want to say farewell to him or our life.'*

It is as well to keep in mind that although the partner left behind will suffer considerably, the one who is off to a new life and a new partner will not get off scot-free either. If you are the one who is leaving, then be prepared for times when you will need to convince yourself that you have done the right thing by turning your back on your spouse. Suddenly you may be unsure about what you had felt was the right decision, and this can be a daunting discovery. What at first feels like freedom and relief from the months leading up to the separation, can also bring with it a sense of remorse and sorrow. This is especially so if your ex lets you know how badly affected and distressed a lot of people are by your decision, and by the break-up. It is hard to share some of these doubts with a new partner who is brimming over with happiness that you are together at last. It can be very hard to be enthusiastically engaged in a new life, when there are still so many uncomfortable ties to the old.

> *'I felt guilt sit on my chest like a slab of concrete. I wanted to go, I needed to go, yet I felt very bad about it.'*
>
> *'I was surprised when I saw how much he was suffering when he actually went. All I could say was "I hope she is worth all this".'*

Can there be a divorce without pain?

It is only in the movies – and in the tabloids – that people seem to move effortlessly from one relationship to another without any apparent heartache or indecision.

> *'I couldn't understand why once I left all I could do was cry. I felt stuck, unable to go back home, but not able to get on living with Julie.'*
>
> *'I was happy to move out and leave them behind. The strange thing was I had dream after dream of how it used to be years ago. I always woke up crying.'*

Quite possibly you may be thinking, 'Good, let him suffer too', but if your feelings of vengeance and revenge go on too long they will prevent your own recovery. Bitterness will delay your chance of future happiness. It may be hard to believe now, but if you can wave goodbye to some of your anger and resentment the dark clouds which surround you will begin to move away. Another way of looking at it – and this may surprise you – is that you are holding on to your anger as a way of keeping a grip on the past. Say goodbye to resentful feelings as quickly as you can. They serve no useful purpose, and indeed work against your recovery.

> 'I felt all I had left was my anger. It took ages for me to see that I kept the awful loneliness at bay by ringing up my ex and screaming at him. That anger went on for a long long time, but meanwhile made me feel alive.'

Now that you are about to divorce, is it possible to break up without even more arguing? Don't forget, too, that things about your ex that irritated you earlier will enrage you now. His trick of 'playing for time' or not responding to letters or messages may well be his way of annoying you even further. It may also be a game you find yourself playing, especially if you have decided you will not give him an easy way out. However, no one wins this two-step dance, and the agony of separating is only prolonged.

There will be many practical questions you will need to talk to each other about. It may seem easier at the time to say, 'Take the lot, I don't care', but you will certainly regret this later. Or you may be holding on tightly to everything. Is this from fear of being left with nothing at all? Or from a sense of desperation that this is the only hold over your ex that you have, and that somehow it makes up for those feelings of helplessness? Or is it from a desire not to let your ex 'get away' with anything? Ask yourself if you really benefit by your refusal to hand over his collection of stamps or his golf clubs? Yet these are the kind of petty issues which add fuel to the fire of many divorces.

To avoid this wrangling over possessions, many men and women pack up and leave when their partner is out of the house, maybe at work. And surprisingly it is the things that are *not* taken that can cause the most pain. The pot you bought together in Greece on a happy holiday, the special book you were both excited by, all carelessly left behind. Small things like these will almost certainly make you weep. Because although from the outside these may seem unimportant details, they will not feel like that to you.

'When he went the only thing he took of mine was the cat. I never forgave him for that.'

'We fought over every single thing. Why not? I wasn't going to make it easy for her to walk out. It had taken us years to put it together, and she wanted to dismantle it in hours.'

Is there divorce etiquette?

The use of the word 'etiquette' in relation to divorce may surprise you, as it does many people. But consider what etiquette means for a moment. It denotes being polite and knowing what to do on different occasions. Patterns of behaviour evolve which help people to feel at ease and it is particularly agonizing not to know what to do in a tricky situation like the fallout from a divorce. Just think of the planning which goes into a wedding: etiquette is of great importance and even the most laid-back family will get clued up about who does what and who is expected to pay for what.

Have you thought, for example, of what you will do with your wedding and engagement rings? After you divorce will you still wear them? If not, what will you do with them? I conducted a straw poll amongst some of the men and women I know who have been divorced and heard of the different ways this was dealt with. The older women still wore their rings, and not only for the reason Annie gave me: 'After fifty years married I couldn't get mine off, even if I'd wanted to!' The younger women had a number of ways of dealing with this very emotional issue. Alice: 'I put mine in the bank, and will one day give them to my daughter.' Paula: 'I sold mine, I needed the money.' Doreen: 'I took mine off in a rage and threw it at him in the street. I went back later to look for it but couldn't find it.' Celia: 'I carried on as before. I was still married in my mind so I wore a wedding ring.' Carol: 'I am still waiting for the diamond ring he promised to buy me ten years ago. So no problem!'

Some mothers found they wanted to have a ring on their finger, but not their wedding ring, so they compromised by wearing another ring to avoid confusion. It is as well for you to keep in mind that even today a ring on your finger does give out a message to other people. Think of the excitement there was when you first showed your friends your sparkling engagement ring. And how you longed for people to notice it and congratulate you.

> *'I went to work without a ring. It was the first anyone knew that we had trouble. It was a good way of announcing it.'*

Men, on the whole, had less of a problem. First of all, fewer men wore wedding rings from the start. But the rest, to a man, had taken off their wedding ring and as Brian told me: 'That was the end of the matter.' Well, yes and no! The symbolic giving and receiving of rings is a very important part of a union, and it is sad that when a marriage fails there are no guidelines about how to go through this untangling of a couple. Most of the women who spoke to me said they had to decide about a ring on their own, and for some it was the first step in making a decision like this by themselves. So, 'etiquette' is not just following convention; it can be more helpful in such situations than it sounds.

Telling the rest of the world

How are you going to tell family and friends about the break-up? Is there a 'right' way to go about it? You may feel reluctant to tell too many people; this could be because you feel that to announce that your marriage is over is an admission of failure on your part. You may be experiencing an underlying anxiety about what other people will think of *you*. It is never easy to tell anyone that a partner has left you. Jane waited until Christmas and sent cards signed only with her name and the children's. It was by the omission of 'Jack' that everyone knew he had gone.

What if you have agreed that there is to be a divorce, and yet circumstances mean you have to go on living in the same home? A familiar scenario for many couples, at least for a while. This potentially awkward situation is more common than you may realize, often caused by financial difficulties. If this is what you are going through you will know already that there have to be agreed and acceptable 'rules'. For that is what etiquette is: an agreed way of behaving, so everybody knows what is expected of them. There are couples who manage to work out a system. And indeed in earlier periods before divorce was so widespread many couples managed to use this complicated style of living as a way of surviving. Agreements were made about who would do what. It was a way of putting up a front to the outside world, so that hopefully the rift would not be apparent. The only way this system can work is if there is courtesy, awareness of the other and respect for the other's privacy. A 'civilized truce' was how one elderly man described to me this way of living with his wife of forty years: 'I know when I can use the washing machine, and the kitchen. We are polite to each other.'

> 'I had to live in the family home until I could arrange to buy another house. During that time she would cook for me, but we did not eat together. That sort of thing has to be agreed upon, and kept to. You both need to know where you stand.'

> 'We shared the house for about a year. It gave the children time to see us as separate people, not a couple, before I moved out. The chief house rule was that neither of us would bring a new partner to the home.'

A dilemma will face you if you are not convinced that the break-up is final. What if you tell 'everyone', and then there is a reconciliation? So, you should select who you tell with caution. If you tell no one at all, the danger is that you will feel totally isolated and this will add to your feelings of depression and despair. If you have children then it is in their best interest that you have a confidential word with the school, as they really do need to be alerted to any stress at home. There is no need to tell them all the details, but most teachers appreciate knowing if there are external factors likely to hinder a child's progress and concentration. This communication with other people who are involved with your children on a day-to-day basis is most important.

What about your in-laws? Most likely the families on both sides will already know something of what is going on. Indeed, not only your own parents but often a mother-in-law or a father-in-law will assume the role of peacemaker and provide a shoulder to cry on. Will the break-up mean losing your parents-in-law and the rest of your ex-partner's relations? Of course, you may decide you don't want contact with them any more, but if you have been a couple for some years this further loss can be a severe wrench. Moreover, family loyalty can be a formidable thing to reckon with, so don't be surprised if there is a closing of ranks, and you are out in the cold. Whether or not the break-up has been dubbed *his* fault it is almost impossible for parents to turn their backs on their own sons or daughters and so you are likely to experience the harsh truth that blood is thicker than water. At no time is this more apparent than when a couple split up.

> *'I left my husband and have few regrets. I did hate hurting my in-laws though. I wrote to them to say I was sorry about the way things had turned out. They didn't reply.'*
>
> *'My mother-in-law was wonderful, she tried to help us in every way she could. But he left me anyway. I miss her still.'*

> *'My in-laws took my side when we divorced. Of course they see their son and his new partner, but they still see me from time to time too. I love them.'*

For most couples the simplest way seems to be just to tell a few close friends, and the grapevine will do the rest. But wait a moment, and think about whether the friends are 'his' or 'yours'? Are the couple you met together on holiday last year going to stay friends with you both? Although friends you shared may declare they will still see you and your ex on separate occasions, this can turn out to be extraordinarily difficult to arrange. The chances are one or other of you will find you are left behind and not included in arrangements. However well meaning people are, they all have busy lives, and juggling the politics of a newly divorced couple may be just too complicated. Especially so if they are privy to intimate details about why there has been this break-up. Embarrassment, and an uncertainty about what to do or say to you, can be a reason for the telephone not to ring. You may be surprised how much it can hurt when you discover that someone you believed was a particularly close friend of yours, gives his or her vote to your ex, and you find you have lost a friend.

> *'I truly felt stabbed in the back when an old college friend of mine asked Bruce to a party and not me. She called me up and asked if I minded. She said he was feeling pretty lonely. As if I wasn't!'*

One more thing to keep in mind: it is not beyond the bounds of possibility that you may meet up with your ex at a social or business occasion. This may be quite unexpected, but try to be prepared for this eventuality. Once again, if all else fails, fall back on being polite, even if you are a bit frosty. Don't see it as an opportunity to have a go at your ex or to tell everyone around you what a pig your ex has been to you, even if it is true.

Divorce etiquette

- Decide what message you want to give people by whether or not you continue to wear a wedding ring.
- If you have to go on sharing accommodation decide on the rules, and stick to them.
- Be polite to each other – remember there was love there between you once upon a time.
- You should try to decide together who you are going to tell about the break-up. When? And how?
- Do remember to let your in-laws know what is happening. It will be appreciated, for remember they may be grieving over their loss of you.
- Don't put friends on the spot: they may have to choose between you and your partner, but let them do it in their own time.
- If you meet by chance months or even years down the road, keep cool. There is nothing to be gained by an angry outburst at this stage.

Everyone gets hurt

Even in the midst of your own confusion and turmoil do try to keep in mind the effect your divorce will have on a number of other people. It goes without saying that any children from the relationship will be deeply affected, and in addition your own parents and family, your in-laws, friends and even colleagues will be touched in varying degrees by the split. Sometimes the shock of hearing about a divorce can shake even the most contented couples into looking at their own relationships. Your distress will stir up feelings, so don't be surprised if you are expected to deal with emotions on their part which often verge into anger. As a result their reactions may not always be sympathetic and supportive.

> *'My father, my own FATHER, said to me, "Oh, you always were difficult to live with". Can you believe it?'*

Carol, who was so hurt by her father's reaction at the time of her divorce, said that it was only years later she could understand what it had been about. She gradually came to understand that he was very distressed to see her so hurt, and that his gruff words actually concealed his own pain and the misery he was feeling for her.

> *'My husband told me he was leaving me for another woman, and my mother-in-law suggested I turn a blind eye. She said she couldn't bear to think of a divorce for one of her children. I hit the roof.'*

Counting your losses

Many losses result from a divorce; they come in different guises and so you need to watch out for them. You may be surprised to find – as many do – that things previously taken for granted are no longer in place. Josie received a note from the tennis club to tell her that as a divorced wife her membership privileges were withdrawn. Although that didn't present a problem for her in itself, the very fact that she was branded as an outsider hurt a lot.

You may not have realized before the break-up of your marriage that there was a certain status attached to the kind of work your partner was engaged in. The sudden drying up of semi-official invitations, or the exclusion from social events previously taken for granted, can all add to your sense of bereavement and isolation. If part of your identity has been augmented by being the partner of, for example, a musician, a doctor or an academic then you will be only too aware that your status has been diminished. You may have grumbled half-heartedly about making the tea for the cricket or bowling team, but there was a comfortable atmosphere about the familiarity of those sunny afternoons. When it dawns on you that all this is going to change you may have very mixed feelings about the total life upheaval confronting you.

> *'I would never have believed I would miss his work 'do's'. But I did.'*
>
> *'For the last year we hadn't had much of a social life together, but we did keep up the wine-tasting evenings. Something I couldn't face going to on my own.'*

Above all, you will experience a sense of loss about the security you believed you had in your marriage. It is fairly common for even the most stalwart person to find that a fear of facing the future will be activated. This may make itself evident in difficulty getting to sleep, or waking in the night with a feeling of foreboding. It can be very scary to be heading towards the unknown when you are at a low ebb and unprepared.

Stress manifests itself in a variety of ways, both physical and mental. So how can you combat this? First of all, identify the symptoms you are experiencing. You may be feeling generally under the weather all the time, or you may be irritable with everyone, or feel you have no energy to fight on. You may have noticed quite rapid weight loss or gain. Newly divorced people all seem to undergo an increase in physical aches and pains. On the other hand, although the repressed emotions often surface in a bodily way, if you are suddenly experiencing unusual symptoms don't just put them down to stress, get them checked out by your GP. Once you get the 'all clear' then you can consider getting some professional help by seeing a counsellor or a therapist. I discuss how to go about this in Chapter Eight.

If a man or woman loses a partner through death, everyone

accepts and understands that the one left behind will go through many different stages of bereavement. No one requires a grieving widow or widower to be full of fun or the joy of living, and yet in contrast newly divorced people find that this is what is expected of them. 'Come on out and enjoy yourself' or 'Forget her, she wasn't worth it. I've got someone for you to meet . . .' These are the expressions of encouragement that you may hear from well-meaning friends. They *want* you to feel better, and may not appreciate that you need time to adjust to all the changes in your life. Too often there is a temptation to respond in similar terms, and to jump to and join in. But there will be a price to pay for this if you do not allow yourself time to deal with the loss of your partner and the tremendous number of changes in your life.

It takes courage to say 'no' to invitations because you may fear they will not be repeated. There is also the feeling that by accepting every invitation that comes along you will alleviate the loneliness of being a single person. Trust your instincts here: if you want to be with people, then go all out to make sure that you are; on the other hand, if you need some solitude to lick your wounds in private, make sure you take the time and space you need. Go with your feelings.

Laurie told me that what he had lost through his divorce was a belief in himself and in anybody else. Before the break-up he felt he knew where he was going in life, and that his feet were on the ground; he felt safe and sure of himself. After his wife abandoned him he was left feeling anxious about everything. 'It was as if I suddenly realized that I didn't know what to take as a "given", and that I had to reassess everything I thought I was certain about.' What Laurie had lost was a sense of trust, and when that is destroyed the uncomfortable sensations that take its place make for very uneasy living.

By now you will have admitted to yourself that with the end of your marriage you have lost your dreams: dreams of a happy life with the person you love, or loved. Hopes of a future together have vanished, together with the expectation that your life together would in time merge into companionship in old age. You will now have realized that broken dreams mean broken hearts.

Are you prepared for the loss of:

- Reflected status from your partner's work.
- The companionship of a partner who has shared a sport or hobby.
- Your sense of security. If this is disturbed, it will in turn affect your peace of mind during the day, and at night.
- Your good health. You may find you are physically less robust than before – there is a strong link between mind and body.
- Belief in yourself as a loveable person.
- Confidence about what lies ahead.
- Your old dreams and wishes for the future.

If you answered 'no' to most of these questions you need to reconsider your position or steel yourself to deal with the future.

Taking stock

If you have been honest with yourself about how you are feeling and you have weathered all the difficulties so far encountered, then it is time to take stock and to assess where you are before moving on. Even if you find you are still on a rollercoaster of emotions, don't worry. Feeling optimistic at times and engulfed in black despair at others is all part of the process of recovery. Remember that in the past you often tried to blank out feelings which were there; they may have been early warning signs which you ignored about your failing marriage and your growing unhappiness. Now with your fresh outlook on life, you are developing the skill of keeping in touch with the ebb and flow of your emotions, so accept this. You are beginning to take care of yourself in a way you have not experienced before in your life. You are learning to trust your instincts and to accept the way that you are. You are discovering how to take your own emotional temperature.

Are you looking after yourself in the ways we considered earlier? Are you keeping a careful watch on your physical and emotional health? It is vitally important that you feel healthy both in mind and body. Even the way you talk to yourself is important. If you find yourself saying 'I need' too often it will in fact make you feel even more impoverished. If you can keep a watch on the words you use you will actually feel strengthened by using positive phrases such as 'I choose', 'I will' or 'I can'. Try them and feel the effect. Are you keeping an eye on your diet and intake of alcohol? If you are taking care over things of this sort, then you are on your way to greater autonomy and personal development.

> *'Bliss, bliss, bliss. I started to buy and eat the food I enjoyed. Gone were the fry-ups and heavy stews. I had forgotten how much I enjoyed fish and fruit. I started to look and feel better than I had for years.'*

If you are living as a single again, you may be dismayed to find out how much your ex contributed to the smooth running of your life. Was it your ex who sorted out the house insurance and paid the tax on the car? That was in the past, this is *now*. So reach out for the telephone and get a recommended garage, or find the nearest dry-cleaners. Think of making a plan for your life. Try to divide it up into short-term and long-term goals. Each time one of these tasks is completed it will add to your sense of well-being and boost your confidence for coping on your own. Crying over a dripping tap or burnt potatoes will do the opposite.

> *'One year on, I realized the only things I missed about my ex was when I had to go to a party on my own, and when I had to deal with the garage about my car. Not much, really, when you come to think of it.'*

The fears that were there so recently will begin to recede as soon as you find you are able to do many of the things your partner used to do for you both. There is a considerable sense of achievement when you have organized and arranged somewhere new to live, and all the planning which that entails. But remember that people on the whole can be very helpful, so do look to others when you need to. Make sure that changes of addresses are recorded, and you may also need to register yourself at a new doctor and dentist and on the electoral role. Even banks and building societies are friendlier these days and will help you to set up a new account or transfer your old one. Don't fall at the first hurdle of car maintenance, or plumbing. Don't wait for the crisis to happen first. There *are* people who can help, so, on an everyday practical level, make sure you keep a handy list of plumbers and electricians for emergencies.

If you have never cooked before now is the time to start. Don't be overambitious: there are books to tell you how to cheat a little, by combining easily bought recipe dishes with fresh vegetables and fruit. Men will find they can work washing machines and dryers as well as women; believe it or not men nowadays even do their own ironing! Don't be like Gordon who for the first two months after the break-up of his marriage bought new shirts each time he needed a clean one.

No one has ever said that living as a single person again after being in a couple is easy. It is not. There will be hours to fill that you never noticed when you were together. Make sure you occupy this time in a way that is most satisfying for you. What about the CDs you never had time to listen to? Do you remember that you gave up going to the theatre because it was not an interest of your ex? Look around you and you will see there are more single people than you thought. It is very easy when in a partnership to mix only with other couples and neglect some of your friends and colleagues because they do not fit in with your life as a couple. Reach out to them now, since this can be a way of building up a fresh network of friends who don't just make you remember what you have lost, but see you as you are yourself, not half of a broken partnership.

Even if it does not feel like it today, you are poised on the brink of new opportunities. If you have children they must, of course, be at the top of your list of priorities but this does not mean you cannot look to the future for yourself as well. Although it may be more difficult with the kids around, do try to open up fresh interests. At the end of the day if you can do this, you will find it will benefit the children as well as you.

The time period for recovery from a divorce, just as from a bereavement, can vary considerably, depending on your character and circumstances. But however wobbly you are on occasions, this is *now* and the moment must be taken hold of and not wasted. In ten years time you should be able to look back at today and say, 'Yes, I was trying to get over that terrible time, but just look at me now'. Remember, you have wings even though they might have fallen into disuse, so try them out, and fly!

Checklist to see how far you have come:

- Are you taking care of yourself physically and emotionally?
- Are you eating well?
- Are you renewing interests which you had given up over the years?
- Are you looking around for new friends?
- Are you building up a 'help' list for emergencies?
- Are you learning new skills – things your ex used to do for you both?
- Are you making a plan for your future?

If you have replied 'yes' to four or more you are entitled to say to yourself 'Okay world, here I come again!'

5

Children and divorce

If we had loved each other so much, then why hadn't it lasted? Was it really impossible for two people to stay together forever in the lousy modern world? And what was all of this going to do to our son?

(Tony Parsons, *Man and Boy*)

A child's view of divorce

You must realize that your divorce, and all that you are experiencing, will be viewed very differently by your children. Although for the parents a divorce may seem to be a remedy for an unhappy situation, it is unlikely that your children will see it in this way: most probably they will feel their whole world is cracking up and they will be left with a desperate feeling of resentment and bitterness. It may be true that by the break-up you are getting rid of some of the problems facing you, but where the children are concerned they are only just starting.

It is surprising, but very often a fact, that for young children divorce usually comes completely out of the blue. This may be because they have subconsciously put up a barrier to block out the growing unhappiness at home. If they don't manage to do that then children may be painfully aware that the two people they love most in the world are at each other's throats. They may then have a grim foreboding that their family is about to change for ever, and not necessarily in their opinion for the best.

The question which will be uppermost in many parents' minds is, 'Will the children be affected by our divorce?' The answer is very affirmatively 'yes'. *How* much they will be affected depends on many things, which is what we will consider in this chapter. The degree to which they will be hurt will be strongly influenced by their experience of family life before, during and after the break-up.

> *'I was not prepared for the way my children reacted to our break-up. We had had an okay family life up until I left and I thought that would see them through. It didn't and I still feel bad about that.'*
>
> *'Do you know, I think it was all the fighting that went on after our separation which really hurt the kids. Up until then I don't think they had known anything was wrong. Seeing us fight tore them apart.'*
>
> *'I wouldn't let them see their dad after he walked out on us. Of course, he gave up trying and they don't have any contact. They blame ME for that.'*

Too often someone in the throes of a new love-affair will block out from their minds the immense pain that the break-up of the family will cause their children. Their hope is that the children will *not* be affected, that they will understand the position, and adjust accordingly. I have heard on countless occasions remarks such us, 'Why didn't anyone tell me my daughter would suffer so much if I left?', 'I didn't think about the kids if I am honest. If I thought about them at all, I did think they would cope better than they are doing . . .' or, with resentment, 'Other children seem to manage' and 'They have friends, other kids whose parents have split up, they are not the only ones, so why the big deal?' Comments such as these show how far we can push the prospect of distressing those we love into the background. And, let's be honest about it, it reveals how adults protect *themselves* by assuming that the children will be 'okay'. If you face up to the burden of how they will really be affected, it could well be that the load is just too heavy to bear. For you to pull out and leave your family involves a considerable amount of guilt and, as we saw earlier, for many partners this is too much to cope with and they find they no longer have the will or courage to depart. This may result in the very distressing scenario of a parent leaving, returning home and then later going away again.

Too many people are lulled into believing that because divorce is now so common, the break-up after a divorce will not be so traumatic as they expect and it will hurt less than everyone makes out. Believe me, there is no basis for this completely misleading assumption. Even the most loving and devoted parents very often convince themselves that their children will not have a tough time of it all, and that they are strong and mature enough to withstand this inconvenient blip in the pattern of their lives. Invariably they soon learn how wrong they are.

So, how can a separation be carried out in a way which eases the pain and distress the children will suffer? Make no mistake about it, children mind very much if their dad or mum leaves the home. Even though they may have sensed the bitterness and tension between their parents, they will nurture the hope that all will be well in the end. So you must set out to ensure that the price *they* pay for the divorce isn't more than they can deal with.

> '*I was ten when Dad left. I thought he would come back. I went on hoping for years.*'

The children are not to blame

Many children blame themselves for the friction at home and react to this in various ways. If there has been a deepening rift between you both as parents, the kids will have felt this and, children being children, they will try to ignore the tense atmosphere. They are sure to know other children whose parents have split up, and they will begin to fear a similar nightmare scenario for themselves.

Whatever you may think, children *do* keep an eye on their parents and they will quickly become aware of anger or sadness, however well disguised, and this will affect them adversely. If you decide to sleep apart your children will wonder why. Don't try to fool them by remarks such as, 'Daddy snores,' or 'Mummy keeps me awake with the light on'. These comments may be believed by under-fives, but older children will see through such excuses and it will add to their sense of unease that something is wrong. Try telling the truth – that you both need a bit of space at the moment.

So many adults I have worked with have vivid memories of lying in bed as children and hearing their parents having a go at each other. In this situation children often misinterpret what they overhear, and all too readily think it is something they may or may not have done. One man told me he was convinced for years that his failure at the eleven-plus exam was the cause of the terrible rows and violence between his parents. Only as an adult did he add two and two together and work out that it was just coincidence that the break-up of his family came around the same time as his school exam results.

If they blame themselves for the collapse of their families and if they can't find a hook to hang an explanation on, children may act out through bad behaviour at home or at school. There is little sympathy in society as a whole for kids who show delinquent traits or anti-social behaviour, but they are often children who are trying to deal with a situation they do not understand and who show their despair by destructive acts. The 'I don't care' attitude which can drive adults wild with rage is so often a sign that a child cares very much indeed.

Ways to help children if parents are fighting each other:

- Don't be afraid to tell the children you are both going through a bad time.
- Tell them you are trying to work something out, if that is what you are doing.
- Do try to keep the rows out of sight and sound of the children.
- Reassure the children that the situation is not of their making.
- Resist the urge to give veiled hints about things they don't know. For example, 'Oh, if only your mother would . . .' or 'Dad could make things better if . . .'
- Watch out for any signs of different behaviour or signs of disturbance in the children.
- Remember their actions often speak louder than words. Take time to be with the children. If there is tension at home they will need you more than ever.
- Remember the way children react after a divorce is partly dependent upon the quality of family life before the break-up.

'I remember when I was ten there was a dreadful atmosphere in the house. I started staying out a lot, and when I was at home I made as much of a nuisance of myself as I could. It was awful from then on.'

'I used to hear Mum and Dad rowing night after night. I know it's silly but I thought I could stop it somehow and that's about the time when I became anorexic. I just stopped eating. It didn't prevent Dad from going though.'

Caring for the children's needs

If you are the parent the children are to go on living with, you may well feel daunted, even terrified at the prospect of becoming a single parent. You may be anxious about coping on your own, and worried that your own feelings of loss will somehow impair your ability to manage. (I look at what it will be like to be a single parent in Chapter Seven.) You are likely to feel resentment that while your partner is off, perhaps to a new relationship, you have been left with children who are disturbed by the break-up and who are behaving in a way that shows you just how affected they are. Even though you accept how difficult it is for the children, you will be impatient with them for showing their distress by being rude, unhelpful and uncooperative, the common behavioural patterns shown by all children when their world is tipped upside-down. Make no mistake about this, the children and their needs must be cared for from the start. You should tell them a little of what is going on, at the same time reassuring them that it is nothing they have done or not done which is making you sad and at times angry. But even this caring and protective approach will only very slightly lessen the impact; the news will inevitably hurt.

An added pitfall at this crunch time is that while every parent wants to get the children on his or her side, the children should not be alienated from their other parent. Immense care and forethought are needed, since even an unsuspecting throwaway remark may make the children, quite unfairly, believe they have to take sides. You may feel that this is what your partner deserves, but think hard about who you are punishing. It can be unbearable for children to hear that a parent has been cheating, cruel and that 'he doesn't want us' or even that 'she doesn't love us any more'. If you put the emphasis on 'poor me' and tell the children in too much graphic detail about why Daddy has left, this could be the beginning of distancing the children from their father. Avoid, too, the implicit suggestion that *they* should be caring for you now that you have been left on your own.

> '*I believed from the start I should tell the kids the truth about their father. They didn't want to hear but it made me feel better. I didn't want them to start going over to his side.*'

Parental Alienation Syndrome (PAS)

In 1985 Dr Richard Gardner gave a name to a serious situation which can and does arise in some separations, and he called it 'Parental Alienation Syndrome'. This denigration of the 'other' parent has long been with us but it now has this rather formidable label, and it can be called into force in a legal battle about custody of the children. It is now accepted that blackmail of this kind, for blackmail is what it is, can affect children so deeply that they become preoccupied with negative thoughts and feelings about the 'other' parent. So, take care that your ex, or his solicitor, does not have grounds to accuse you of Parental Alienation Syndrome. In addition, beware of allegations of sexual abuse, since these can become the ultimate weapon used in issues over contact with the children. You may believe it is unthinkable that accusations of this kind could be made, but when the situation gets fraught between you and your ex and solicitors are involved anything can happen, so take any hint of PAS seriously. Make sure that accusations of this sort or any other kind cannot be levelled at you.

If you are on the receiving end of PAS and the children say they do not want to see you, make certain that you keep as much contact as you can. Be sure to keep records of how you have tried to communicate with them, and keep in touch with as many people who do have contact with the children as you can.

At its most extreme PAS can end in abduction, with the children professing hatred for a parent they formally loved and needed. Even if there is not a physical abduction, parents can be accused of 'abduction of the mind'. There is plenty of evidence being gathered to show that this unhappy state of affairs is more common than we would all like to believe. Most children of divorce will continue to love both parents, but where PAS creeps in there is no chance of them being able to maintain a loving contact with both of them. Pamela S. Stuart-Mills has become a renowned expert on this unhappy family condition. The Rachel Foundation, started by Stuart-Mills in 2000, is dedicated to reintegrating abducted and alienated children with their families, and monitoring research that supports these efforts. Her dream has been realized with the opening of the International Reintegration Center. This is where a previously denigrated parent can slowly become reunited with a child. Visit the Rachel Foundation website (www.rachelfoundation. org) to learn more about this work, generated by the pain of families torn apart by abduction or alienation. The foundation is in Maryland USA but they are not able to publicise their telephone number or address because a large proportion of the cases they are working with hold a high risk of re-abduction.

Recognition of PAS is gathering momentum. In the UK 'The Equal Parenting Party' (www.equalparenting.org) has been formed with the sole aim of fighting for 'equal rights for parents'. This body has been instrumental in bringing to the public's (and the judiciary's) notice the unfairness of many family situations. They campaign vigorously to prevent the widespread growth of PAS. 'Families Need Fathers' (www.fnf.org.uk) is another organization which has plenty of information about this syndrome, so get in touch with them both if you feel this is what is happening in your family. FNF welcomes mothers and also grandparents.

Precautions to avoid damaging accusations being made against you later:

- Be on the alert for changes in your children's behaviour towards you.
- If the going gets tough, don't let it just ride: if you are not allowed access which has been agreed mutually or through the court, take action as soon as possible.

- Get legal advice.
- Keep detailed records of how and when you tried to see the children.
- Don't give up.

Telling the children about divorce

All children will want to know what a divorce will mean, how it will affect them, and what changes are likely to take place. How you tell them will depend on their ages and the particular factors affecting your own situation. The best way is for both parents together to tell the children about the separation, in a way they can understand. But even parents who both accept that this is the way things should be handled often fail at the job because what the children will be told has not been worked out in advance. The moment when this is going to happen must also be thought about. It cannot be left to luck. If it is, then the chance something will be blurted out in the heat of the moment increases a hundredfold. Couples who spent months planning every detail of their wedding, neglect to put the same amount of care into their divorce. Yet it is especially important that painstaking care is applied to every aspect of a divorce if you are parents.

I have already said that the best way to help the children is to be together as parents when you break the news to them, yet I am aware that this is not always possible. If you are on your own then careful preparation is all the more important, because you will be setting the scene for the future relationships in the family. If you have fudged over the issue of why the other parent isn't at home – 'Dad is working away for a bit' or 'Mum has gone away for a rest' – then it could be difficult to tell the children the truth now. You will have to explain to them *why* you told them that. It may be that you were unsure yourself about what was happening, or perhaps you gave your partner time to decide whether or not to come home.

They need to feel that they can trust you now to tell them the truth about what is happening to the family. Keep in mind that if you have children of different ages, you may need to have a further word with the older children later. Indeed, it is a good idea to give each child a little private time with you alone in order to answer any questions which they may not have liked to ask with the others present.

'We agreed to tell the kids together and do it the "right" way as parents. When the time came he didn't turn up, so the kids heard my version of it all. We all huddled in a heap and cried and cried.'

'Oh, how I wish I had protected the kids from seeing their dad leave with his suitcases with us both red in the face from shouting. They were both white from shock.'

'Yes, yes, yes, I know now how we should have done it. All thoughtful-like – but you should have been there, it was hell, pure hell.'

'Tell the children? I couldn't even tell myself that the marriage was over.'

Of course if the family has been in chaos for some time, then the separation is likely to be chaotic too. But, if at all possible try to agree together what and how you will tell the children. Listen to what they say too, and have answers ready. Don't be afraid to say, 'I don't know' if they ask you something you cannot answer. This may be in reply to a question which you judge relatively trivial, but it may be of supreme importance for them, such as, 'Will Daddy come to my concert?' In answering questions on more fundamental matters try to be as honest as you can without overloading them with details. If a parent is moving out, or has already gone, the children will need to know where he is living, whether they will be able to see that parent and if they can visit.

Prepare yourself for your children's reactions. Even if you are forewarned, it is going to be difficult and painful ground to cover. One child may appear not to hear at all, and just seem to get on with what he is doing. Another may run from the room in an attempt to deny what is happening. Yet another may break down with grief or burst out in anger. It may be that you will find that *you* are on the receiving end of their fury, which is extremely hurtful if you are the parent who is telling the children something you would rather not have to let them know! You will need to brace yourself for their reactions, and you will need to keep in mind that telling them is only the start of helping them understand and face the collapse of the family and all the difficulties that go with it. In no way is it the end of the matter. Talking will go on for a long, long time. They will need to be updated as the situation changes, and you will find that issues you thought had been clarified will have to be gone through time and again.

Of course, it is not only young children who may have to be told the news of the separation of their parents. 'Adult children', who may even be parents themselves, can be shattered to the same degree when told what is happening.

The cruelest of all blows is if you have to tell a child that the other parent has gone and you don't know if or when you can arrange a meeting. I am afraid this does come about all too often. If this is what is happening to you, it is important that you still tell the children the truth and don't try to protect them by lying. For instance, there are parents who cannot deal with the disappointment felt by their children when the expected birthday gift from an absent father or mother does not arrive. However, giving a hastily wrapped present to fill the gap merely prolongs the fantasy that there is another loving parent 'out there'. After this the fall, when the truth is eventually discovered, can be utterly devastating.

Explain to the children some of the difficulties which mean that the marriage cannot continue, especially if they themselves have been affected by them. It will also help the children if, over the next weeks or months, you can speak of past happy times too. They will need to be reassured that the family they believed they belonged to previously did, in fact, exist. Children need to be reminded of the good times because they will get comfort from remembering when all was well between their parents. Make sure there are some photographs around too of happy family occasions. Do you have some early photographs of you all, perhaps taken within minutes of a birth? Tell the children that although the family is changing and in the future things will be not be the same, it is not the end of the world, and that together you will cope with the differences. It is the best you can do.

'I tore up all the photos with her in the moment she left. I regret that now, and have since been glad my parents kept some and I can let the kids have them.'

How to tell the children about your divorce:

- Try to agree as parents what, when and where you will tell the children.
- If your partner will not cooperate, decide for yourself.
- Vow you will not make your child 'take sides'. Nobody wins that round.
- Choose a moment when you are not rushed and can give the children plenty of time.
- Tell them in an age-appropriate way – this may mean giving older children additional information separately.
- The children will need to know about the break-up – you cannot protect them from this.
- They will need to know how it will affect them.
- They will need to know about any changes which are going to take place, immediate and long term.
- Do tell the truth. Don't think you are protecting the children by fudging issues.
- Don't put all the blame on the other parent. Remember to the children Mum is Mum and Dad is still Dad.

- Ask them if they have any questions. If they don't, they will come sooner or later so be on the lookout for them.
- They may ask 'Why?' This will be the hardest question of all to answer. It will not help the children to tell them all the details of a sexual fling or other 'adult' reasons.
- Think over in advance how much, or how little, you plan to tell them.
- Don't be afraid to cry – it *is* a sad time for the family!
- BUT, the children will need to feel that you will cope and be there to look after them. So keep your deepest grief and sense of betrayal away from the children. They have enough to cope with without looking after you.
- Avoid saying: 'You will have to take Mum's/Dad's place.' These words will weigh very heavily on a child and are unfair.
- Let the children know which friends and family members you are telling, and give them some guidelines about who they should tell. They may need to talk to their friends, so don't make them promise to keep it a secret. Tell them, though, about discretion and privacy.
- Do tell the school, playgroup or any carers of your children about changes in the family. Enlist their help in observing the children and noticing their reactions.

The importance of keeping contact with your children

Even today, when there is so much talked and written about the importance of both parents keeping contact with their children, there are still some who feel it may be kinder to make a clean break and not to stay in their children's lives. This is a big mistake. If both parents can appreciate this then it will be easier for them to be flexible and make arrangements for the children to remain involved with both mother and father.

> *'Okay in theory, but my ex-wife moved with the children over two hundred miles away. I went to see them for a bit, but it was so awkward – everyone ended up crying or shouting. It was best for me to keep out the way. I will get in touch when they are a bit older.'*

This is a sad comment from Rob and his choice of words is revealing, '. . . my ex-wife moved away'. Yes, indeed she did! Without the support of a husband, Rosie, with two children under three years of age, moved back into her parents' home, both for support and for financial reasons. Rob seems to have no understanding of the impact the loss of a father has upon the children: 'Best for me' he tells us. It is *he* who cannot stand the upheaval and distress caused by seeing the wife and children *he* initially moved out from. He comforts himself with the thought that he will just go back into their lives 'when they are a bit older'. The reality is that they will be two children who do not know him, but this does not seem to have penetrated his way of thinking. There are many dads who slip away from the family for their own reasons. These men continue to give fathers a bad name. The press are quick to have a go at 'dead-beat dads', but there are still far too many different reasons why a parent loses contact to speak in such general terms.

There has been a great change in opinion concerning the importance of the father's role in a child's life. Now, when men do decide to leave their wives, fewer are prepared to 'divorce' their children too. A lot depends upon a father's involvement before the break-up: a father who is used to taking the kids swimming, reading to them, and generally enjoying being a dad, is now far less likely to take a back seat, even if he is the one who wants to get out of the marriage. Many mothers are not prepared for this, and assume that they will automatically have the major say in all aspects of childcare. Times are changing, and nowhere more speedily than in the acceptance that dads have rights too.

Of course, if you are still in shock you will not find it easy to adapt to an ex who asks you for arrangements to suit him and his new partner. This will affect your feelings about whether or not to make it easy for the handover from one parent to another. So this is truly a time to grit your teeth and give priority to what is best for the children. Remember, access is for the benefit of the children and not for the convenience of either you or the non-residential parent.

> *'Funny, arrangements about when he can see the children are the only thing we never quarrel about. I'm really glad about that.'*

You will need to agree on guidelines about how you hand over the children from one of you to the other. It is most important to understand just how crucial those moments are to the children. They will be looking to you both for clues about the way you treat each other. Anything you need to say which would be painful for the children to hear, should be said on the telephone. The golden rule should be if you can't say anything good to each other in front of the children, say nothing at all. This will be harder to stick to than you can imagine.

The physical 'handing over' from one parent to the other needs to be sensitively handled. You may think I am crying for the moon when I urge you to make it as smooth as possible, especially as it may be a time when you can hardly bear the sight of your ex. I have heard of too many children being 'swapped over' in the dark, in motorway cafes, or pushed out of the front door which then closes rapidly behind them. It is cruel for the children to be made to bridge the gulf between two parents who are at loggerheads. However much you are hurting, however much you loathe your ex, he *is* the children's father and for that reason alone deserves some courtesy. Nowhere is this more visible and demonstrable than at handover time.

> *'We never say bad things to each other at handover time. We do it at other times on the phone.'*

It may be that after a while the handover can be extended to include a cup of coffee too. You will almost certainly find the children love that. If you can even manage a meal together occasionally so much the better; it will reinforce for the children what you have already told them – that parents divorce each other, but not their children. If you have accepted that it is important for the children to keep on being involved with both parents this will help you to come to the table in a conciliatory mood, whatever your real feelings about your partner are. By actions like this you can both combine to rebuild the children's sense of security and they will benefit from this.

> *Joe came to put Michael to bed two nights a week. It worked for us. I would go to the gym knowing Michael was happy. Friends found it so difficult to understand though. They used to say how can you have Joe back in the house. Seeing Michael's little face made it possible for me to do so.'*

It is not unusual for a mother to find she has to help smooth the path for a child to go on a visit to his father and vice-versa. Young children may be afraid that if they go to the other parent, the one they live with will have vanished when they return home. A great deal of reassurance by both parents is needed here. Wise parents will also try to gauge the length of time for visits at the beginning, and will not insist on keeping to 'my share' if a child shows signs of distress or is homesick.

Decisions will have to be made about *where* the non-resident parent will see the children. Will Dad become one of the growing army of fathers wandering around the zoo until it is time to return home? Will you welcome your ex into your home to play with the children, and even let him put them to bed sometimes? Will you be happy if your ex wants to take them to his new home where he may be living with a new lover? Will you go together, or separately, to school events? What if one child wants to go for a 'sleep over' and the other does not? These issues, and many many more, will come up – some sooner rather than later. Each one will need to be considered separately. Guard against an automatic 'no' if a request is made. Don't feel, either, that you have to say 'yes' immediately. Give each issue the thought it needs.

> 'I was frantic: when Paul wanted to go and see his Dad, Daniel didn't and vice-versa. I never knew whether to make them both go or not.'
>
> 'I made my children make a solemn oath they would never go to their father's new house and meet "her". I told them it would kill me.'

Try to keep any discussion about the children and the arrangements direct and to the point. There is nothing to be gained by inserting a dig against your ex when you are in the middle of a negotiation about an event even though it may be on the tip of your tongue to slip in a remark such as, 'I didn't think you would turn up, you never used to be interested,' or even, 'Don't be late again, you never could keep to the time agreed'. Possibly you have bitter memories of being kept waiting over the years by your ex but if you are genuinely trying to smooth the path for the children then hold back, and accept that this is not the time to be at war with each other.

It is better for the children if they can keep to as much of a routine as before. If Dad has taken them to football practice each weekend, is it going to be possible for him to continue to do so? This continuity of parental care can be especially important if the children have been used to extended family occasions. Look out for the first major holiday after a separation; this can be a tricky moment. What if the children have been used to spending Christmas or Thanksgiving with your in-laws? The issue here is whether you can bear to be parted from the children on these days of family celebration. But stop and ask yourself what is best for the children? Different couples come up with different answers, but the happiest solution for the children is when you both give some time to being 'parents' for them; even though this may be for short periods, this is better than two adults at war over them. Can you consider overlooking your own hurt and welcoming your ex into your home so that the children can open their presents with both of you there?

> *'Just after Paul left it was Maggie's birthday. I invited him back to see her cut the cake, but he was late and it all ended in another row. Never again.'*

You may feel I am asking too much of you even to suggest this. It might be the hardest thing you have ever done. But if you can let the children stay where they will be happiest during the holiday period, you will have the satisfaction of knowing that you are keeping their lives on a steady path . . . even if it means you weep alone. Again, and I feel I must repeat this, if you are into punishing your ex, slamming the door on him will only increase the pain for your children.

Guidelines over contact and for access:

Whether the children are living with you or their other parent the guidelines are the same.

- Communicate with each other about arrangements, not through the children.
- Agree if at all possible that decisions about finance and similar matters are NEVER discussed in front of the children, especially at handover time.
- Disagree all you need to on the telephone or even face to face but not in front of the children.
- Remember that access is for the children, so try to put your convenience second.

- Don't change arrangements already agreed to. Ask yourself who you are punishing if you back off from plans which have been made.
- Be flexible if possible. It helps the children if there is some leeway all round and they are not shared out strictly fifty-fifty between the two of you.
- If you are going to be late, telephone to say so.
- Keep to the agreed timetable. Don't interfere with this as a way of getting at your ex.
- Whatever the flak, try to keep in mind that you are parents and behave appropriately.
- Avoid any hint of 'poor Mummy' or 'poor Daddy'. This is not fair.
- Keep firmly in mind that children need both parents. Even though it may go against the grain, if it's you who has to make all the arrangements for your ex to see the kids make sure you do.

Shared care

'Shared care' is a way of parenting after a divorce which is gaining ground with some parents, so you should be clear about what this means. In the US the term 'parenting time' is being introduced to cover both 'shared parenting' and 'shared care'. I like the use of this term, because up until now 'shared care' has often meant dividing the child's time in a way, perhaps as much as fifty-fifty, which is not necessarily in the child's best interest, whereas 'parenting time' implies a much more flexible approach. I feel it also puts the spotlight on what it is all about – time to do some parenting.

As much as I believe that children need two parents, I am not convinced that strictly divided time is the answer. I have seen too many children who spend a week with Dad and a week with Mum becoming disorientated and uncertain where home is. On paper, an arrangement of this kind may look ideal. The child may or may not have a room in both homes, but would you like to be 'on the road' for such a large part of your time? Would you like to have to decide which of your treasures to move with you each week? I cannot help feeling that this arrangement is often to soothe the parents, rather than the children. Many people will not agree with me, and if this arrangement seems to suit you and your children, then go for it. But do watch out for the children's reactions as they cope with contrasting rules, set-ups, and even food!

> 'I hated it when I was a kid. Mum liked things done one way, and Dad the other. I suppose that's why they got divorced in the first place. I am sort of used to it now.'

Shared time should be as much for the convenience of the children as for the mums and dads, although this is not how all divided parents like to see it. All regular arrangements, such as that the non-resident parent will have the child each weekend and a part of each holiday, must be open to change when necessary. What seems to be okay in theory gets skewed when the children begin to have their own arrangements and plans. What happens then? The wisest parents, of course, do bend to fit in with birthday parties, matches and other events which are so loved by growing children and very important for their social development. One of the saddest comments I have heard from an adolescent was, 'After the divorce I never had any time just to hang out with my friends'. So do keep this in mind when dividing up the children's time between you.

Here is an instructive if somewhat extreme case history: Jake insisted that his son should make a flight of over 300 miles for two long weekends each month. Jake felt this was the way to keep contact with Paul, but what he got instead was a reluctant and weary schoolboy who was unwilling to enter into any of the plans his father had made. This arrangement failed eventually because Paul developed mysterious 'stomach pains' every other Friday. It is sad to see that Jake's plans, made with the best will in the world, did not fit in with what Paul needed. After a few months Jake tried again, this time consulting both his ex and Paul. What was agreed was that Paul should visit each half-term and for longer in the school holidays. This was a success, but the sad fact is that many fathers would have become discouraged with the result that contact could have broken down for ever. If there is a moral here, it is that you should make sure you use your share of 'parenting time' in a way which suits you all.

Keeping in touch

The idea of 'parenting time' appeals to me for several reasons. First, the non-resident parent does not always have suitable accommodation for the children to stay overnight. But this in itself should not rule out involvement in daily activities. If it is geographically possible both parents should arrange to share some of the fetching and carrying duties which seem to be part of bringing up children today. This also keeps both parents up-to-date with details of their children's lives. It is the 'Sunday parent' who is at sea about who is the latest 'best friend' while a parent on a school rota soon learns about the ups and downs of school life.

Distance can be a problem, but it is easier to keep in touch today, since there are fax machines and e-mail and long-distance telephone calls no longer cost as much, and of course there is still the traditional post. By establishing regular contact from the start using one of these methods, it soon becomes part of a child's routine. And children do need routine. They need to know the plans for contact, and let me emphasise once again that it is very, very important for the parents to keep to agreed schedules and plans. Children who are already bereft will feel even less valued if arrangements are cancelled because you are 'busy' or 'just can't make it this week'. Routines should be established as soon as possible after the break-up. If the children are not living with you, make sure these arrangements don't get left on hold for the time being. It is easier if you establish a plan from the start, rather than trying to set one up later, so be sure your voice is heard over this important issue.

> *'Learn from my mistake as a father. I was so depressed after my wife left I just let her make all the plans. I came off badly.'*

Beware of adolescents baulking at arrangements made on their behalf. Enlist input from them wherever possible. It may be that a child wants to assert independence or even use his power of refusal to cooperate as a way of signalling disapproval about the separation. Try to be patient, because whether they like it or not, adolescents really do need parents. So, if your teenager is refusing to see Mum or Dad, try to help him over this hurdle. He will be too inexperienced to see ahead and realize the disastrous effect that not keeping contact with both parents may have on him in later life.

One more point about helping a child move between parents: give a child time to settle down again when he or she returns home. It won't always mean they are unhappy, or that they don't want to talk about the visit. But it is important that there is a little breathing space before the child moves back into family life at home. Equally, if you are the parent who does not live with your children, give them time to be at ease with you when you meet them. In fact, don't try too hard. There is no need to always be 'doing' something with them. A walk by the river or a board game is just as important as getting tickets for the latest show. What counts is time together with you. Keep in mind, too, that whether you call it 'shared care', or 'parenting time', at the end of the day it should add up to the same thing: continued involvement in your children's lives as well as taking on your share of responsibilities.

> *'We managed okay as a family. My advice to others? Play fair, and don't give the non-resident parent impossible schedules or tasks.'*
>
> *'After the divorce what I lost was just loafing around the house and garden with the kids. A pizza? No big deal then – now it takes two lawyers to fix it up.'*

Shared time:

- From the start agree with the other parent what 'shared care' means to you both. You may have very different views about it.
- Don't settle for less than you feel is right for the children.
- Agree to be flexible, within reason. Don't see 'shared care' or 'parenting time' as just time to amuse the kids. Take your turn in ferrying them around or with trips to the dentist or for a haircut.
- Keep in touch at other times too.
- Don't change arrangements which have been made unless totally unavoidable.
- Be fair – stick to times agreed.
- Don't let the children feel that arrangements are made only to suit the parents' social life.

Keeping an eye out for disturbed behaviour

If you feel that your child is withdrawn and falling back on school work, first of all talk to your ex about this. Find out what, if anything, the other parent has noticed. Your child may find it easier to talk more openly to one parent than the other. This may or may not be the parent he is living with, so it is important to find out. It can be very upsetting to be told by your ex that your child is, 'Fine, no trouble at all with me'. This implies that *you* are the problem. Whereas the reverse may be true and it is only in your company your child can let go and be free enough to show his feelings.

The next step is to talk to the school. You may be pleasantly surprised at the help and support they will offer. Some parents hold back from this resource because they still don't want 'everybody to know our business'. Yet the children *are* the school's 'business' and so the staff will want to help you to support them in every way they can.

If moodiness or rudeness goes on for too long, don't put it down to 'being an adolescent'. You will have kept an eye on your child's mental health during the break-up, but now that everyday life has found a new routine you are less vigilant. You may not want to believe it has anything to do with your finding a new lover, so you will be inclined to turn a blind eye to the gradual unhappiness of your child. Adolescence is a fraught time for many children and if you see your child struggling, you should get some professional help. (I have found that many adults undergoing psychotherapy report clearly knowing they were depressed as teenagers, but being amazed at the same time that no one seemed to notice!) Your child may initially kick against the idea of talking to someone, but talking to a stranger who is experienced in these matters can help a lot (as it does for adults) by providing an ear to listen to stored up resentments. Ask your doctor or clinic for a referral, or consult the resources in Chapter Eight.

Signs of disturbance in your child:

- Trouble at school, perhaps unruly behaviour or concentration problems.
- Is your child 'comfort' eating, or perhaps not eating enough? Watch out for rapid weight increase or loss.
- Does your child burst into tears for no apparent reason?
- Is your child more isolated than previously? Are friends still calling around and phoning?
- Is untidiness or rudeness 'just being an adolescent' or is it a sign of more serious inner turmoil? Talk to the school, talk to your ex . . . and talk to your child!

Your divorce and the grandparents

The pain of your divorce not only affects you, your ex and your children but other members of your family, too, particularly the grandparents. Whether they are your parents or your in-laws, whatever happens will affect them deeply. It will be a sad and difficult experience for them to see the family they thought and hoped was safe and happy, begin to splinter.

When there is a divorce it is startling to see how quickly lines of demarcation can be drawn, so take care over this important issue, because it is not only your own relationship with the grandparents which is at stake, but the relationship between all the generations. In the middle of the upheaval and the changes to your day-to-day life, do spare a thought for your in-laws. Don't punish them too. It is painful enough for a child to lose a parent, but more so if half of the extended family vanishes as well. It may not have occurred to you, but at the time of a divorce most grandparents have their hearts in their mouths at the thought of losing their grandchildren, which is something that can happen all too easily and quickly. There are more bereaved grandparents around than is readily acknowledged. If the children are with a parent who is not all that close to her in-laws, or caring towards them, then the extended family link is likely to be broken. In some cases, of course, it may be your own parents with whom you are at odds.

'I had no warning of the searing pain I would feel when I heard my daughter-in-law was leaving my son. It was the worst time I have ever known. I felt so helpless.'

'When I heard they were breaking up, all I could think of was "Oh, those poor wee babies!" That made me cry.'

If you are a grandparent and one of your offspring has been badly hurt by his or her partner, it may be hard for you to keep in touch with your daughter-in-law or son-in-law, since you will almost certainly feel that in this way you will be supporting the very person who has brought about this family split. The result is that in this situation your own child's children will lose the support network they are so much in need of.

Again, remember that battle lines in a divorce get drawn very early on, so if you are a grandparent in this position you must behave responsibly. Make it clear from the start that you want and intend to keep being involved in the children's lives, no matter what the cause of the break-up or whose 'fault' it was. Whether your son or daughter becomes the resident parent or not, any support you offer is likely to be most gratefully received. But accept that there is a limit to what you can do. Let it be known, by all means, that you are there to be called upon, but think carefully about jumping in and offering more than you can cope with. In the heat of the moment many a grandmother has offered to take on part of the care of the children, but this is not always easy to maintain. The other side of the coin is that you may find yourself drawn into the position of offering a base for the non-resident parent to see the children. In this way you may find you see much more of the grandchildren than you did before; the single-parent family may be very happy to share part of the weekends and holidays in your home.

Mothers who leave their children

Remember that from the start I said that in this book 'mum' and 'dad' are interchangeable. Nowhere is this more apposite than when discussing parents who leave their families, because it is *not* always the father who goes away. On occasion mothers leave their children and when they do, they seem to have a much harder time than the men. I am at a loss to explain why an adulterous man is often regarded as a 'bit of a lad', whereas women in a similar situation are seen in a much less tolerant light. Mothers find they are subjected to scorn in a way men are not, and people have no difficulty in speaking their minds about the contempt they feel when they hear a woman has left her children. 'Unnatural', 'callous' and even the milder criticism of 'How could you!' are hurtful words thrown at mothers much more often than at fathers.

> '*As soon as people know I left my three kids they look at me as if I have committed a crime.*'

Women who collect under the umbrella of one of the support organizations like 'Mothers Apart From their Children' tell harrowing tales about why they had to leave their children. Seldom, if ever, is it for a careless or frivolous reason, and yet the stigma remains. Sometimes a mother makes the supreme sacrifice and moves out because she has faced up to the grim truth that, for whatever reason, she is totally inadequate as a mother.

> '*I moved out. In due course my ex remarried and the children are in a happy and secure home. I pray that in the future the children will understand. I am quite alone and I still suffer from bouts of severe depression. I have learnt never to tell people I had children.*'
>
> '*I had to leave my husband, but every day of my life I pray I did the right thing leaving them with him.*'

Why should the world treat mothers who leave their children in such a cruel way? Is it because we all like to carry an image of an all-loving, self-sacrificing mother figure in our hearts? A mother who will stay with us forever against all odds? And to hear that a mother can leave her children destroys this image for us? If you are in any doubt about the misery for so many of these mothers, then read Penny Cross's *Lost Children: A Guide for Separating Parents*. Her knowledge of the pain of mothers separated from their children is first-hand. When she left her former husband she found her children cut her out of their lives. She says she did not abandon them, just a husband and a miserable, failed marriage which had lasted twenty-five years too long. In Penny's own words: 'Naively, I didn't question that leaving their father could impair my relation-ships with my children in any critical way. It didn't occur to me their feelings towards me could be so vitally affected or so gravely influenced ... Prepared to console and support them throughout their misery, I found I was not needed – being apparently the reason for it.'

Her book was written to warn parents of the potential risks of just walking out on their marriage or relationship, leaving ill-prepared children behind in the family home. Her intention is to alert everyone to the real possibility of their children becoming irreversibly brainwashed into believing, if they are left behind, that the parent who has left has abandoned them. Cross tells what it is like to be on the receiving end of PAS. So even if you feel you are acting in the children's best interests to leave them in the family home, you are running a high risk of losing the children. Don't bank on the children putting all their anger on the break-up. It is likely to be directed at you. As Cross found out, your estranged partner and your children may appoint themselves as judge and jury. The verdict? You have been a failure as a parent because you apparently abandoned them.

> *'I knew I had to leave, but I had no idea my children would feel abandoned. I expected too much of them to understand. He had the money, the house, his parents' support and I thought at the time I was doing what was best for them. I should have talked to them and prepared them but I just couldn't. We all paid a high price.'*

It is estimated that over 150,000 mothers live apart from their children in the UK. Some because a marriage to a foreign national has ended and the children are abducted. Another reason is children not returning from a holiday abroad with the other parent. If you are a woman in this position, expect a shocked and abusive reaction from people if you tell them you are not living with your children. You may find to your distress that explanations can sound like excuses. If you are still grieving over your separation from your children, be warned that a harsh and insensitive word will be felt as an extremely vicious blow.

Beware! Guidelines for mothers leaving their children

- If you are a mother and you leave your children, you are likely to be given a hard time by society.
- The reason you left may be poverty, abuse, depression, not enough information about your rights, or a hundred other reasons. The 'world' will hear only that you left your children.
- Even if your children are abducted you may *still* be given a hard time.
- Don't assume children will realize why you had to go. They will feel only the pain of your departure.
- Don't expect their anger to be focussed solely on the divorce.
- As a parent, you have to take responsibility to prepare your children for your flight.

6

Domestic violence

We are effectively destroying ourselves by violence masquerading as love.
                                                                    (R. D. Laing)

Abuse in the home

Violence in the home is one of the most common reasons for a break-up. A quarter of all reported violent crime in the UK is domestic. This abuse knows no boundaries of class or religion, and is seldom visible to the outsider.

> *'It was so gradual-like, the times he hit me. I never knew how it got so bad until he broke my arm.'*

Violence, in one form or another, may be there from day one of your relationship. For other couples it can gradually evolve from some other battle between you. It may even break out sporadically without warning in an otherwise okay marriage. One of the hardest of all situations is when there is a swift transformation from a loving partner into an aggressive, controlling and punitive one, and then back again, with remorse and promises of change in the future.

Perhaps you associate 'violence' with a black eye or other physical injuries. Many women do, and so they fail to identify abuse when other forms of violence enter into their relationship. It may be quite insidious, beginning as a barrage of threats and ridicule which escalates over the years. It may take the form of raised voices or shouting; these are types of bullying. Many men seem to be unaware that women on the whole react badly to harsh and abusive language. If you are a man, you may feel that you have been on the receiving end of vitriolic words, but somehow they do not seem to have quite the same impact on men as they do on women.

Violence is about power, and this can be about controlling a partner by either physical or emotional abuse. Sex is frequently used as a way of dominating a partner. Violence can even begin in bed in a joking kind of way, and then take root in a more oppressive manner; it is not always easy to spot the point where the line was crossed and sexual 'games' became sexual abuse.

> 'We used to have a lot of fun in bed, but he began to go too far and I got badly hurt. The first few times I told the doctor some lies, but I don't think I was believed. No one offered any help though or asked me questions.'

Accusations of jealousy, adultery, or even stupidity may be hurled at you, and as many women can confirm, verbal abuse can be as hurtful as being thrown down the stairs. Attempts at fighting back may bring further violence: tears of frustration and helplessness are ridiculed or seen as a sign of 'weakness' instead of a reasonable and healthy reaction to the situation. Sometimes there is a warning about what is about to happen, and many partners learn to observe the signs which are triggered by drug or alcohol abuse.

> '*I was so ashamed. I used to cover up my bruises and I never told a soul what was happening. I look back now and see I was a fool.*'

Don't be misled into thinking that violence is always about the man abusing the woman. Men are victims too, and the accompanying humiliation makes it equally hard to bear or to break free and seek help.

Facing up to violence

Abuse can take many forms, and is always about control. Not all abuse is physical, and the verbal abuse which wears down a partner's self-confidence can be psychologically very damaging. If you are told by your partner that you are useless and worthless this may contribute in time to your feeling, and believing, that this is so. The result will be a severe loss of self-esteem. And this in turn will make it extremely difficult to change the situation; it will be very harmful if you have children since they will have to watch a parent being continually belittled and humiliated. Unfortunately, in these situations you find you are so worn down that you cannot summon the strength to do much about it.

From the outside it is hard to understand why a partner stays in the home when he or she is subject to abuse. And yet men and women often let the situation continue for years, frequently going from bad to worse. It may be that the abuse has slowly escalated, and it is easier said than done to shout 'enough'. There is not a great deal of information from professionals to help people out of this desperate situation but this is beginning to change. As you will read in Chapter Six more helplines and agencies are aware of the problem and are reaching out to women who may be isolated and the victims of domestic abuse. The Metropolitan Police in London are running a campaign urging anyone who needs help, or knows of someone in distress, to contact their local Community Support Unit. This information will hopefully raise the public's awareness of this often life-or-death issue.

There should be no sense of shame if you have to say to an outsider, 'I am being beaten' or 'I am shouted at day and night' or, 'I am married, so how can I accuse my husband of sexual abuse, yet that is what it feels like'. It is much worse to keep up a wall of silence, not telling family or friends and waiting in anticipation for the next incident of abuse. According to some agencies forced or arranged marriages have more than their share of domestic strife.

> *'I knew our marriage was dreadful from the start. He wouldn't talk to me about how unhappy I was. I think he knew I didn't love him. He insisted on sex without contraception and I got pregnant again and again. It took a long time for me to see that as abuse.'*

Children and violence in the home

When children witness their parents' marital conflict and discord, their sense of emotional well-being is harmed. A child in its inner world, from a very early age, constructs a view of how 'the grown-ups' manage the ups and downs of life. If children see endless fighting and arguing between parents, especially if it escalates into violence, they will be scared by what they see and hear. If, on the other hand, they learn that heated discussions can be resolved and the other person's view, although disagreed with, can be respected, this will go a long way to helping them establish successful relationships later on.

Recent research (*Childhood Experience of Domestic Violence* by Caroline McGee, published 2000) shows that children are very much aware of any violence and not fooled even if one parent attempts to conceal it. If you have been on the receiving end of violence from your partner don't try to hide it from the children. Your motive will be to protect them, but children are not easily deceived, and they tend to catch on to a situation far more quickly than most parents like to believe. It is best to bring it out into the open and let other people know and get professional advice about the whole situation as soon as you can. Both for woman and men it is always a big step to begin to tell friends or family that you are the victim of violence at home. The whole family will be gravely affected by abuse between partners. Children become reluctant to bring friends home in case violent behaviour is evident while they are there. Studies also show that where there is violence in the home, children cannot concentrate on work at school and so failure there is added to their sense of the failure of their family life.

> *I didn't know what to do when Dad started yelling and hitting Mum. She used to shout to us to go upstairs but I was scared he would kill her.'*

If you have been in this family situation then you will know how hard it is to protect the children. Although there is now more government funding for refuges for women it is still difficult to find counselling and other support for the children. Some parents persuade themselves that they should put up with the situation, believing that the children are not being harmed, and the status quo is better than a family break-up. However, as already stated, children are quickly aware of trouble between parents. Often the final straw comes when the abuse is directed at the children, and then somehow the parent finds the strength so say, 'No more!'

The fear is that the social services will get wind of the situation, and judge you as not being a fit parent. Anxiety about the children being taken into care naturally looms large. You may feel that because you have children it will be difficult or impossible to find somewhere to live. But you must get advice and find professional help. Above all, talk to your children about what is going on and what you are trying to do about it.

Complications arise when the abuser says he loves the family very much; this seduction is often what has kept the family together for so long. The threat of suicide 'if you leave me' is not uncommon.

This kind of blackmail, for that is what it is, must not be used: you must get help to recover from the months or years of attack, for no one should have to live under the threat and fear of another.

Looking for help

Fortunately, there is better legal protection in the UK now. Or is there? And how accessible is it to someone in deep trouble? I was told that it was now easier to apply for an occupation order which gives the victim the right to remain in the home. Yet, when I telephoned the Metropolitan Police's new helpline I was told it was very difficult indeed to get, and in answer to my questions I was 'advised' not to go down that road. I asked about the non-molestation order and the reply was equally vague and unhelpful. 'Come in', I was told. 'Next time you have bruises we can photograph'. Was any counselling and support on offer for anyone exploring this avenue? This question was met by silence and then the suggestion that I should telephone Victim Support, who although they don't do 'domestics' are 'really very good, and might help'. I was given their number and that of the press room of the police at Scotland Yard who I was assured 'would be very helpful'. Sadly both my calls to these numbers went unanswered. I visited our local Police Shop in person asking for information. I was directed to our local Police Station, which had closed over a year before!

So, although I am told that there is more police awareness of what used to be dismissed as 'domestic' crimes, my own research shows that help is not easily accessible for one of our most vulnerable groups of men, women and children. I can only hope that my experience was unrepresentative of help across the board. A later search in the neighbourhood library gave information about some very local help offered by Women's Aid. So keep looking! There *is* a non-molestation order which is there to provide safer protection, and can stop one person pestering, threatening or being violent to another person. However, you have to be fairly robust to travel that road. You should make a start by contacting your local magistrates' court or county court for information.

If you have been on the receiving end of violence, you must seek maximum protection and support for yourself and the children. The Women's Aid Campaign works tirelessly to focus attention on the abuse which so many women suffer. Their work is dedicated to 'a future without fear'. That certainly doesn't seem too much to ask in the year 2001, does it? And yet the statistics available show that we only know about the tip of the iceberg concerning domestic violence. Are you someone who is finding what I am saying all too familiar? Quite likely you have experienced violence, for as many as one in four women experience domestic violence at some stage in their lifetime, regardless of ethnic origin or social status.

You may have been thinking for some time about leaving. You may even wonder why you have found this hard to do. This could be for many reasons, but the main ones stem from love and fear. Love, hoping against hope your partner will change, can be a strong reason for staying. Feeling you can understand what drives him to violence and believing you are the only one who can help him may make you reluctant to leave him. This can be especially so if there are times when your partner is weeping with the shame of what he has done to you. Perhaps he still begs you to stand by him. And you do, even when trying to cover up your own bruises. As time passes you may have found that you have withdrawn from family and friends because you found it increasingly difficult to explain away certain marks. Eventually this contributes to the difficulty of leaving since you feel there is nobody you can turn to for help.

Fear: you may be terrified that if you do leave, he will find you and injure or even kill you. Indeed, this threat may be part of the abuse which you have been suffering. Also, you may be frightened that if there is any sign that you are even thinking of leaving, your partner will turn on your children. Another threat which causes fear is that if you leave he will not let you have the children. Maybe you are simply scared of the future on your own. Again, if you have children, how will you manage, where will you go, and how will you find the physical and emotional strength to go? Where will you live, and what will you live on?

Safety first

These must be some of the questions which go round and round in the head of anyone experiencing domestic violence. Women's Aid suggest you make a crisis safety plan to help keep you, and any children you may have, safe. They suggest you store emergency clothes, money, special children's toys, important documents, addresses, telephone numbers and duplicate car keys with someone you can trust. If you decide to move away by yourself make sure it is safe and that your partner will not be able to track you down straightaway.

The first step is to believe that you do have the right to live free from fear of violence and ill-treatment. You know that physical violence can result in permanent injury and sometimes death. You know that mental pressures and emotional abuse contribute hugely to the number of women who suffer from serious depression. The second step is to believe that you can change your life. To do this you will need some help. You will need advice about your legal rights, protection, safe housing and money. Don't waste another moment before seeking advice.

A last word of warning: don't take it for granted that a divorce means the automatic end to abuse from your partner. You will still need to make sure you are protected.

> 'I know that even though we have split up, when he is into drugs anything can happen. I have had to break off all ties and start a new life. From fear, that is. Thank God we didn't have any children.'

If you are a parent, you will have the added responsibility of seeing that your children are protected too. If your ex wants to see the children you, and they, will be safer if you find a place where visits can be supervised. Make enquiries at your local social services.

Signs that you are being abused:

- Does your partner unjustly accuse you of all manner of 'crimes'? These 'crimes' may be as innocent as spending too much time talking to a neighbour or family member.
- Are you constantly trying to avoid situations which are likely to provide an 'excuse' for an outburst.
- Watch out for the gradual escalation of violence in a relationship.
- Do you feel under threat of violence?
- Have you been physically harmed?
- Does your partner try to have a hold over you by controlling sex or money?
- Is your freedom curtailed? This can be either through physical or mental control. Are you constantly asked 'what are you thinking'?
- Do you have to 'account' for time away from home?
- Does emotional, verbal or actual physical abuse play a part in your relationship?
- Have you been 'warned' not to talk to friends and family about your 'accidents'?
- Do you feel blackmailed by threats of what will happen if you leave your partner?
- Are the children witnesses to violence?
- Do the children live under fear of violence – either to themselves or to you?
- Is your partner's erratic behaviour dependent upon drugs or alcohol?
- Are you seduced by repeated promises of change?

. . . and remember

- There is no shame in asking for help and protection.
- Domestic violence is a crime, and should be seen as such.
- You will need to protect yourself even after a separation or divorce.
- Leave nothing to chance when it comes to the safety of yourself and your children.
- Don't abuse yourself by taking the blame.

7

The new family

Meeting your partner's ex should be awkward and embarrassing. You know the most intimate details of their life and yet you have never met them. You know they did bad things because you have been told all about them and also because, if they hadn't done bad things, you would not be with your partner.

(Tony Parsons, *Man and Boy*)

Introducing a new partner

Red warning lights should start flashing when your partner tries to juggle arrangements to suit his new love. This can be very hard for you if you are still trying to come to terms with his betrayal and adultery.

> *'The thing that hurt was when he said he never wanted them on a Saturday because that was the only day he had free to spend with HER.'*

If you are preoccupied with the details of reassembling your life – and this may or may not include a new partner – it is not unusual for a parent to go along with the dream that the children will absorb the changes. If you have a new partner you might even be hoping that the children will welcome him into their lives since he is the new person you have grown to love. This is one of those difficult stretches when your children may not be uppermost in your mind, and you may not sufficiently take into account their feelings. You are likely to be overwhelmed as you deal with the 'adult' issues you have on your plate, and the children are moved into second place for the time being. Watch out for a hazardous pitfall at this time: when to introduce a new partner to your children. This always requires extremely delicate handling. But all too often the heady excitement of falling in love again makes parents rush into it so that they precipitate the moment of introduction. There is an old saying that 'a love and a cough cannot be hid', but all the same you should go extremely slowly at this point. If the introduction happens too early on and without careful thought, tears are likely to be shed by you all. If this first meeting is a disaster, and all too often it is, it can be the start of a family rift which will continue for years, perhaps for ever. Your expectations for yourself, your partner and your children must be realistic.

'I couldn't have believed how awful my children were the first time I had a date. I could hardly recognise them. Later I was furious with them and let them know it.'

'But I was moving in with Libby, and the kids needed to meet her.'

Did they really need to meet Libby the same week as they were told that Dad was moving out, that they would be moving to a new home, and when they saw Mum crying almost non-stop? This is an area which needs great sensitivity and tact. Remember, you may have grown to know and love your new partner over a considerable period. For the children the news of her existence probably came out of the blue and they will need time to absorb the shock and grasp what it all means. All children know stories of wicked stepmothers, and you will not be doing your new partner or your kids any favours by projecting this image on to her. Of course, in time they must meet her, but you need to take responsibility for choosing the right moment. Springing a meeting on them will start things off on the wrong foot.

Make time to talk to your children about what is happening and prepare them for a first meeting. Give them time to get used to the idea, and if they seem less than keen – leave it for a while longer. They will also need to be reassured that he or she is not taking the biological parent's place, even if in your heart you hope differently. So, don't try too hard to bring everyone together at this time. Your main concern should be the effect the split is having on the children, and there is no need to burden them further with the introduction of 'someone else'. Remember that the children will already have torn loyalties and will be trying to come to terms with them.

If you live with the children, then the time will come when you begin to think more seriously about a new relationship. But again you must tread carefully. If your children meet a new boyfriend at breakfast then they are likely to be shocked. They will be even more confused if he doesn't appear again!

'I had a brilliant idea when I wanted Max to stay the night. I told all my kids I was having a sleepover and Max would be staying. They didn't think it was at all funny, so we decided to leave it for a bit until they were ready.'

On the other hand, if they have become used to 'George' around the house on a Saturday, perhaps giving you a hand with some of the chores, they will have had time to make up their own minds about whether they like him or not. But it may be altogether different when you give a hint that your feelings for 'George' are getting more serious. They have probably enjoyed having you to themselves, and the prospect of sharing you again may not seem so great. But take care not to pass over to the children the power to decide who you may or may not be friends with. It really is unwise to say something like, 'Do you like him? No? Right, I won't see *him* again.' As well as cramping your style, it gives too much responsibility to the kids.

> *'I really regretted telling the kids when we first broke up that I would never marry again. Five years on I met a lovely man, and the kids kept reminding me of what I had promised. So be careful what you say in haste.'*
>
> *'I made sure that the children understood I was in love again, and that meant I was happy with a new partner. No way was I looking for a new dad for them.'*

You may, as a new single parent, have decided to keep your social life quite separate from your family life. If the time comes when you know your feelings for a new friend are becoming strong and serious, then you should look for ways of introducing him gradually to the children. Hopefully the kids will feel more settled again, and although they may at first be jealous, and fearful once more that their life will change, with the right approach from you and your new partner they may see there are some benefits as well. The key is to give everyone time to get to know each other; this is something which cannot be forced or hurried. If he is just a 'good friend' and you sense that your children are concerned about whether he is about to turn into a new 'Dad', reassure them that this is not in your thoughts. They may find it good to have a new 'friend' too, particularly if he has some skills which appeal to them, like mending bicycles!

> *'When Mum met Graham she was in a better mood, and didn't keep on at us so much. He's okay, I suppose.'*

If *both* parents are each involved with a new partner, then the difficulties increase; the children will be even more unsettled. There will be less space in either parent's minds for them, and so the effect of the break-up may linger. Children do get depressed. This is a fact which surprises many adults but sadly depression in children is quite common. So look out for this.

> '*The worst time was when Dad had Kath, and Mum met Eric, and we used to hear them rowing about who was to have us on a Saturday night.*'

How to introduce a new partner:

- Take your time. After all, if you plan to be with your new love for a lifetime, what is the rush?
- No one can step into another person's shoes, so reassure the children about this.
- Give the children time to get to know the new person in your life.
- Use some discretion. Take some time before the children are faced with a new man at Dad's place at the table, or a new woman bustling about in Mum's kitchen.
- Remember the children will be fearful of the prospect of a *step*mother or *step*father.
- Don't force the pace, so be sensitive to the children's – and your new partner's – needs.

Are you the new partner?

What if you are the new partner waiting to be introduced to the children? What can you expect? And what will be expected of you? When you fell in love and you knew there were children from a previous relationship, did you think you would all get on together without any problems? Perhaps, as the moment got nearer, you began to wonder if it would be 'alright on the night'? Or did you not know at the beginning of your love affair that you were getting involved with someone with a young family? Once you were aware that there were children in your partner's life it may then have crossed your mind that in some way your life would become entwined with theirs. This may have filled your heart with joy, or horror. Did you talk over with your new lover how this introduction would come about? And when? And where?

I heard from one young woman, Charlotte, who fell in love with a man with a five-year-old daughter. The little girl lives thousands of miles away in the US and they have only all met up once. Charlotte told me that because of the distance involved she is able to 'forget' about the girl's existence for most of the time. But she dreads the thought of the child coming to stay, even for a visit. She asked me why I thought she felt so strongly antagonistic towards a five-year-old. It is not the child alone that causes her so much anguish, but rather that the child is the living embodiment of her new partner's earlier relationship. Charlotte seems to have entirely blocked this out from her consciousness. If this sounds like something you can recognize in yourself, think carefully about how you should cope with a lover who has a child from a previous relationship.

The hardest situation of all is to have your new partner's children with you, when your own children are not. How do you explain this to them? Of course, they may be perfectly happy living with the other parent, but the very thought that you will have someone else's children living with you, but not them, will be a profound cause of resentment. So be prepared! It may be difficult for you to think of living with other children when you see yours only at agreed times, or not at all. One of the most agonizing scenarios for a parent is to become a full-time stepparent when you are only a part-time parent for your own child. When there is a chance of your becoming an involved and committed stepparent be ready for your feelings to be stirred up in a most unexpected and dramatic way, particularly if you are not in touch with your biological children at all.

Alternatively, if you are the partner of a parent in this situation, how can this affect you? Well, you should be aware that although your lover may have agreed to leave his former partner, and you have been supportive about the difficulties, you may not be prepared for the overwhelming feelings he will have when it comes to leaving his children too. Parting from the children can become such a grave issue that you need to be prepared for hitches, delays and even a complete change of heart at the last moment.

> *'I knew I had to leave Polly. I honestly didn't think how hard it would be to tell the children. I didn't want to divorce THEM, but Polly made it all so difficult. I suddenly saw it was going to take much longer to leave than I had first thought.'*
>
> *'Harry said he would take on my children too and I thought that was wonderful. What we hadn't bargained on was my ex saying that he was going to keep the children.'*
>
> *'I was very willing to take over the care of the children from the start. Yet my new live-in lover didn't go for that. Once I met the kids and saw how difficult they were I understood why.'*

Meeting the children

If you are to meet up with the children, and they already know that Mum or Dad is leaving the family because of you, then I am sure you will be ready for the flak which will come your way. You may feel this is grossly unfair if you have met your new partner *after* the break-up of the family. But, to the children, *when* you met is unlikely to make a difference.

Perhaps you are already a friend of the family, and believe that as the children know you, they will slip easily into the new relationship. Don't bank on this. It is one thing for them to see you as 'Barbara', the neighbour or close friend of their parents, quite another for them to see you in a totally different, intimate role. In this situation it can be more awkward for them to have to accept you as the new partner of their father than if you were a stranger. If they are used to you being around it will make them think back to the times you were all together, before the news, and they will be furious to discover something was going on all the time and that they were not aware of it. Even if the 'children' are adult, don't expect or rely on getting 'adult' reactions to the break-up. Any child, of any age, will be feeling their loyalties pulled in different directions. Frequently anger, which they would like to direct towards their parents, may be aimed at you.

There are marriages which have staggered along 'until the children are older'. Today there are women, as well as men, who feel that they will not stay forever in an unsatisfactory marriage. But if this is something you can identify with don't make the mistake of thinking your partner's children will be less shocked now than they would have been ten or fifteen years earlier. Although the children you are about to meet may even be parents themselves, you still won't get an easy ride. What may arise in this situation is that although you may not have children of your own, in one fell swoop you are heading towards becoming a stepparent and at the same time a *stepgrandparent*. This is enough to take anyone's breath away. If this is what is happening to you, spare a thought for your parents: it could be a huge surprise for them to find that overnight they have become stepgreatgrandparents!

If the children are slowly getting used to you it will be doubly hard for them to get to know new grandparents, uncles and aunts and cousins right away. Go slowly. Success will also depend upon the age of the children, and whether they live full time with you. If they only see your parents once in a while it will be some time before any bond can possibly grow between them. It will require patience, and this is something that grandparents are often good at. So don't rush your parents, or the kids. The two generations will probably do best left alone to find a friendly meeting point – perhaps over a shared activity or interest. Keep remembering this is all part of the process of loving someone who is already a parent.

'I am only twenty-seven, but my stepdaughter-to-be is nineteen and pregnant. I can only laugh at how absurd it must seem.'

If you are in a similar situation, consider that it may not seem so amusing to your stepdaughter-to-be. Adult children find it difficult to take on board their father marrying someone only a few years older than themselves. It will be hard for you to understand if your wonderful lover – who you thought had eyes only for you – suddenly becomes so traumatized by the reactions of his children.

'My new partner's eleven-year-old won't meet me, and so every weekend he has to take her to stay at his parents'. They are finding it a strain because they are in their late seventies. I am on my own every weekend. I am worried our relationship won't survive. What should I do?'

This is the kind of e-mail I receive on my website (www.family onwards.com) all too frequently. I find it hard to know where my deepest sympathies lie: with the eleven-year-old, with the father – torn between different loves, with the new lover waiting in the wings, or with the grandparents who are being drawn into this painful tangle of relationships? Let alone the little girl's mother who is also on her own at the weekends.

Even if your lover has left his family *before* you came on the scene, the shadow of the 'old' family will still be there, and there will be much to negotiate with the children. If they have been used to having Mum or Dad to themselves you will be seen as an interloper, however discreet and sensitive you are to their feelings. Children who have been through the upheaval of a family break-up are especially vulnerable when they sense more changes on the horizon. It will help you to get a fix on how the kids might be feeling if you can find out from your partner whether other new 'friends' have been introduced to the children in the past. If there have been others before you, the children may feel they do not have to make any special effort with you since, like the others, you will vanish from the scene. They may even have grown fond of a previous new someone, or they may have waged war and been triumphant when that someone disappeared. Either way, you will have that history to cope with as well.

If you have not had a child of your own you may have to wrestle with your own strong feelings of anger and despair when you are told that there is going to be one more family outing, and that you are not included. You may be itching to get your hands on the children and to show them what a nice person you are, but be guided by your new love. After all, the man or woman you have fallen in love with is trying to balance all the different people in his or her life. Have some sympathy for your partner over this; he may have had no idea how difficult this would be. While this is going on, however much you don't want to think it, the children are a priority at the top of the list and you are second. Try to accept that this is so. If you do not, there will be tensions and heartache. Don't try to get your lover to change any childcare arrangements in an effort to 'prove' their love for you. You will not win that one, and will only stoke up the fire of resentment.

Beware, too, of encouraging your partner to stop seeing the kids, however turbulent it all is. You may well be feeling jealous of them and the time they take up. You may also hate to see the way your lover is being treated by his family. If you are honest you may be feeling a bit guilty over this: it is as a result of loving you that your partner is now on the receiving end of so much anger and hate from people who once loved him. You may also have strong feelings about your new love seeing his ex at handover time. Take the long view here if you can. Although your partner may be getting a hard time from his children and his former partner, if he pulls out now and does not keep up contact and maintain his relationships with his children, in time you may be on the receiving end of a great deal of bitterness and grief. Always keep in mind that your lover is a parent as well. And was a parent before you came on the scene.

Hold on to the fact that you have fallen in love with someone who already has parental commitments, and who honours them. All part of the package, you might say. So if your new partner cannot accompany you to the works' picnic because of a school match planned for the same day – do the adult, loving thing, and try to understand why. After all, if you both plan to be together for the rest of your lives there will be other occasions. The alternative, making your new partner choose, will almost certainly end in tears. Probably yours. When you do meet up with the children try not to rush anything. Don't come on too strong, and although you may be filled with panic, just try to be your usual self. Forget that you are trying to please your lover, and try to dismiss any lingering feelings that you are on trial as a future stepparent and the children hold all the cards. Accept that probably you are *all* nervous about the meeting, so it is best if you have some kind of outing where the focus can be on something other than *you*: a visit to an exhibition, a museum or a zoo. Remember you are there to get to know them a little, and for them to get to know you. Forget the daunting prospect of 'the kids' and try to see each as an individual. This is especially important if they are of very different ages. Most important of all, DON'T tell them what to do and DON'T correct them in any way.

> *'The first time I saw Jamie and Pattie I made a terrible mistake and told them off for not washing their hands. It took years to recover from that early mistake. At the time, I thought it was the right thing to do. Now I know better.'*

This tiny mistake was probably read by the children as 'she wants to be our mother'. Recognize that you are not there to take anyone's place, or to step into anyone's shoes, but as a friend of the children's mother or father, and convey the message that you would rather like to be the children's friend too.

What may seem embarrassing to you may be just straightforward curiosity on the part of the children. Be ready to be grilled. A question such as, 'Are you going to marry Dad?' when you haven't yet been asked, may send you ducking for cover, but keep in mind the children will be anxious to know what is up and what is likely to happen. Make sure you and your partner have agreed what the children are to be told at this stage and what it may not be appropriate for them to hear yet, like whether you are already living together. Remember, children usually think their parents are too old for sex anyway. The introduction of a new person who is so obviously in love will force them to see a parent in a different, often uncomfortable, sexual way. So be tactful about showing too much physical affection in front of them at first. Don't rub it in in the mistaken belief that it will reinforce the message to the children that you are there to stay.

Do's and don't's when meeting the children:

- Don't force the pace – wait to meet the children until your partner judges the time to be right.
- Don't try too hard.
- Don't take it upon yourself to correct the children in any way.
- Don't be surprised or disappointed if the children's feelings or activities come before yours.
- Don't lie – but do agree with your partner before the meeting what you will, or will not, tell them.
- Don't have a go at your partner if the children are rude to you – remember they are also finding it difficult to adjust to a new situation and relationship.
- Don't give up!
- Do be polite – you are setting the scene for the future.
- Do respect their feelings, and expect them to respect yours.
- Do be friendly . . . and tactful . . . and discreet.
- Do give your partner time alone with the children.
- Do judge when it is time for you to back off.

- Do make sure you and your partner have some private time alone too – as a couple you are the core of a new family and need combined strength.
- Do accept that compromises and agreement about how to spend time are essential.
- Do accept that it will take time for you all to feel at ease with each other.
- Do make sure you tell your partner that you love him – he or she may be feeling very battle-scarred.
- **. . . and most of all NEVER criticize the other parent in front of the children.**

Stepparenting

If you are to be a stepparent what can you expect? Are there any rules or guidelines? How can you get rid of the stereotyped image you or the children may have from the stepparents in novels or films?

It will help you to ease into your role as a stepparent if there has been plenty of planning and *talking* between you and your partner about the whole family picture. Make sure you both have the same realistic expectations. The role can be particularly hard to take on if there is not much of an age gap between you and the stepchildren. Even if you are as comfortable as you can be with this, the child – especially a daughter – will find it hard to see her father with a woman fairly close to her in age. All the old oedipal feelings of jealousy will get stirred up, so watch out for this. It is as well to remember that even the most loving mothers and daughters often have a falling out at this time. So don't blame yourself for everything that goes wrong between you. Just acknowledge to yourself that this closeness in age must be hard for your stepdaughter.

Young new brides often make the mistake of thinking, 'Okay, we will just be best friends, then,' but as I have heard time and again, best friends don't arrive just like that. So be patient, and see what kind of relationship can develop between you.

> *'I didn't know what his children wanted. I tried being a mum, and that failed dismally. I was told, quite coldly and bluntly, "We have a mother, thank you". On the other hand, when I tried to have a girls' night out with them, they turned that down too. Just a polite "No thanks". No explanation, and no apology, just "No thanks".'*

A wedding, second time around

If you have worked hard on those first meetings, and not jumped the gun but gradually built up your own relationship with the children, what next? This is the moment for 'The Wedding'. No matter how long a couple have been parted, the news that one of them is remarrying can be a momentous time for all the family. The children will finally have to let go of any remaining hopes that their parents will get together again. The date set for the wedding puts the lid on those dreams. You may be astonished to be told that they hold on to any thoughts of parental reconciliation, but they do. It may not be openly spoken about, but it is there somewhere at the back of their minds. They may be holding on to a rather rosy picture of how family life was when they were younger – before dark clouds gathered over the family – and memories of happier days will nurture a wish that the clock could be turned back. This could account for sudden changes of mood which often perplex adults. After a good day spent together you may find the children suddenly become sullen and silent. You may be asking each other 'What did we do?' The answer is probably 'nothing', but something may have jogged a memory for them of earlier times, and accompanying feelings of loss and sadness can make them ill at ease. Especially if the trigger rekindles the betrayal of the other parent. The remarriage of a parent is going to be one of those times.

The same will be true for the ex-partner, who is sure to have strong feelings on hearing of the forthcoming event, often much to his or her surprise. So it is important, and kind, to tell any ex-spouse of the planned wedding. However long a couple have been separated it would be heartless to let the news come from someone else. Tell the ex before you tell the children. This is especially crucial if the children live with that other parent, as cooperation will be needed to see the children through this additional jolt to the pattern of their lives.

How will you tell them? It is important to convey your decision to them together with your new partner, as this imprints upon them that this is how it is – you are once more going to be part of a married couple. Don't duck out of this one. It is surprising how many couples do, and then they are surprised when the children don't take to the marriage. I hear of parents who still think it is acceptable to tell their children about the marriage after the event has taken place! However tempting this may be for you if your new spouse is a first-time bride or groom, it really will not be worth it in the long run. If your children hear the news belatedly it will be something that the new family will almost certainly not recover from. Even if it is your partner who decides that this is the way to go, the blame for this is going to be laid at your door.

For the person soon to be married for the second time, this can be a period when memories and indecision are to the fore. However complicated arrangements were for the first wedding they multiply a thousandfold second time around. Do keep this in mind. Although you may be engrossed in the preparations for the day you have dreamed of for years, your partner will be more likely keeping a watch on their kids and, as a loving parent, will know what a devastating effect the wedding and all its preparations will have on them.

An important point to bear in mind for the one remarrying: make sure your new partner doesn't feel that this time you are treating the wedding as second best. Of course it will be different, but it must also be very special. So be sure you show your enthusiasm for all the plans being made. Keep this in mind if you would prefer a quiet, informal ceremony while your first-time bride or groom has different ideas. This is where you, as a parent already, and the future stepparent will have some careful thinking to do. It might well be that at this time the ex begins to create all kinds of difficulties. Even an unconscious reaction to the news may result in sudden changes being made to childcare arrangements at the last moment so as to cause maximum inconvenience all round. When you also remember that the children may, once again, be feeling torn in different directions, then you will understand why the stress rises considerably.

> *'Would you believe it? We told her I wanted a June wedding. So what did she do? Announced that she was taking them to see her parents in New Zealand in June. Chance? I don't think so.'*

Why do people do such cruel things? One reason is because if there is still a hangover of pain, grief, or just plain anger between the couple then this tit-for-tat business will continue. If an ex feels that all the cards have been held by you up until now, then hearing of your wedding plans may stir up feelings of revenge, and present an opportunity for them to put a spanner in the works. You may have learnt to your cost that for many couples the legal divorce is only one step along the way to a couple becoming separate again. You may remember, as pointed out earlier, that many men and women cling to their anger towards their ex as if that is all they have left. The pain of rejection lingers a long time. I know that one bride-to-be found this very hard to understand.

> *'Whenever there is peace, either my future husband or his ex will start up a blazing row over nothing, it seems to me. I don't understand it. What do they get out of it?'*

I believe that this young woman was picking up a frisson that unfortunately can still be there between a couple, long after the official parting of the ways. It can only end when one or the other says 'enough' and refuses to play that dangerous game any more.

'Oh dear, children at the wedding?'

You are likely to ponder over whether there should be children from your partner's previous relationship at your wedding, especially if you yourself have not been married before. There are completely divided opinions over this issue. A second marriage ceremony where there are children of one or each partner is not the same as a first wedding for two people who want to celebrate their union in public. It should be borne in mind that a second wedding in these circumstances is about the creation of a new *family*, a stepfamily. To exclude the children from this ceremony is to court disaster. They need to witness the marriage if they are to move towards accepting that Mum or Dad has a new partner. So, if you and your partner can resolve this *before* telling the children about your decision to marry, you might be ready to talk over with them how they would like to be included on the day. They may need time to think about it, and probably to talk to the other parent. So be patient with them, although you may be longing to firm up your plans.

What if one child wants to come and take a very active part, and another does not? A wise parent and a stepparent-to-be give time for the dust to settle and space for a child to change his or her mind. This is where the cooperation of the other parent is paramount. A child may feel it is the ultimate act of disloyalty to take part in the wedding ceremony, and will need the gentle reassurance that this is not so. I realize that I am often spelling out an ideal and things may not go smoothly, especially if there is antagonism between the parents; people being what they are an ex may use this time to tug at the children's heart strings. But if you have a blueprint already in your mind it can help you to foresee, and to negotiate, some of the hurdles ahead. If the answer is still 'no' and a child does not want to come to the wedding, then respect this. By all means say how disappointed you both are, but there is no winner if someone is forced to attend a ceremony. Believe me, no wicked fairy from the storybooks ever cast such a pall over a wedding as a child who does not want to be there and be part of the remarriage of a parent.

There are many different roles that children can play at a wedding. A wedding should be a lovely relaxed day, so again, don't try too hard. If there are going to be children at the wedding, an authentic family affair, then try to allow room for some spontaneity. If the children are already living with you they will probably quickly become very involved with the preparations. Either way, value their input and suggestions, even if they come up with an idea which is unusual. Encouraging them to help choose the colour of the flowers, or the music, will help them to feel truly part of the day.

> 'My stepdaughter-to-be came up with the idea of us walking back down the aisle to the music of "It's a wonderful world". We started to say no, and then my fiancé and I realized just what the message was from her. A truly marvellous wedding gift from her to us.'

If your partner's children are going to take a prominent role on the day, and they live with their other parent, then it will ease things all around if there is room for compromise. Make sure that you do not give the other parent extra responsibilities or financial outlay. If there are travel arrangements, then you should make them, and bear the cost. You should not expect the former spouse to have to get involved with buying 'specific' shoes for the day, or paying for a haircut, or any of the hundred and one things which have to be done before a wedding.

It is wise to talk over with your partner whether or not you should be in touch directly with his ex, since this has particular significance when he has children. His previous wife may well appreciate knowing something about the new woman in her children's lives. No one would really expect you to become bosom friends, but if there can be an affable meeting it will help the children's relationship with you. If you do see or speak with the ex it is probably wisest to keep to the topic of the children. Take the lead from your partner, after all, no one knows better than an ex-husband or wife whether it would be an agreeable meeting or not. If you don't get together, at all costs avoid sending coded (or not so coded) messages home with the children. That will only enrage the other parent even more.

Have you thought what will happen if the children are very small and need to be dressed? By whom? Don't expect very young children to be looked after by relatives or strangers, however kindly and willing they are; they are unlikely to allow themselves to be put into unfamiliar clothes in an unfamiliar place! Hopefully you will be able to have a dry run with them earlier, in order to explain to them exactly what will be happening, and what you want them to do. Make sure that there is a designated person to watch over them all day. They are sure to be feeling a bit lost, especially if it is a large function. This way you and your bridegroom, or bride, can get on with being just that – the bridal couple.

> 'My ex is getting married again in May and my children are excited about being bridesmaids. I want to be there to dress them, but the bride says no. She has said that I can't even see them afterwards because they will leave their clothes there. Is there anything I can do?'

My reply to this e-mail was that there was very little to do in a practical sense. There is no 'place' for an ex-partner, although if these little girls are very young, the bride might wish she *had* let their mother dress them. The best Paula can hope for is a photo of them in their wedding finery. Meanwhile it was good to hear that Paula is trying to make the day as pleasant as possible for her daughters. Telling them in advance that she won't be at the wedding but that she will be collecting them, will go a long way to helping them know what is happening. Another mother in this situation may not have put the children's happiness first, and if there was still a hangover of resentment towards the other parent, may have talked the girls out of being present at the wedding. You might also be asking yourself if it would have been so terrible to let the ex dress the children? Some brides can be generous in this way, others feel that they need to make a stand on this day of all days, with the right to say, 'No, I would not be comfortable with that'.

With older children who can make up their own minds you will, of course, get varying reactions. You will find that almost always the response of the other parent will affect their attitude towards you. But adolescents may have strong ideas about what they will or will not wear. If you object strongly to their idea of wedding clothes, what should you do? Treat it as lesson number one about being a parent! There are always, in every generation, arguments about fashion. Don't you recall having those very same rows with your parents?

If one daughter is happy to wear flowers in her hair and a dress you have chosen and the other is not, then let one walk with you in the bridal party, and the other may much prefer to make her token protest in the crowd. Just try not to let the issue become a battleground. Does it really matter if your fourteen-year-old stepdaughter-to-be wants to wear her favourite trousers which make you wince? You may earn her undying gratitude if you understand that this is the only way in which she feels she has some control over what is happening to her life. Think about it: she may not be out to ruin your day, but may want to find a way of coping with the remarriage of a parent. Just remember that you are the adult here.

It is not always doom and gloom, so take heart: I hear of many very happy occasions where the children have been delighted to give away the bride, to be best man or woman, or to join in a chorus of 'We do' when there is the question of 'Who gives this woman?' Many couples like to give the children a special gift on the day as a symbolic reminder of the importance of the ceremony for them all. Also, make quite sure that there is at least one family wedding photograph with everyone included.

Have you thought about the honeymoon? And the children? Yes, they need to be thought of even at this point. If you are lucky, you may get away as a couple for a while, and you probably think you deserve that. But watch out for your new spouse's feelings too. What will you do if you sense that a 'family' holiday is on the cards, and not the romantic honeymoon seen in the movies? I have heard of couples who agree that as they are now a new family, *of course* they all have to be together. If the children live with you this may be how it works out anyway. If the children return to the other parent at the end of the day, this may not be an issue. But check it out well in advance. Don't make assumptions.

Are there 'second-wedding' manners?

There is still little guidance about post-marriage etiquette, so although we have now had a look at how you should get to know the children of a future spouse, and how to deal with the ex-partner, don't forget that there may also be ex-in-laws, former joint friends of your partner's and an ex who may be on the wedding invitation list. How will you feel about them?

> 'I wouldn't have anyone at my wedding who had been at my future wife's first wedding. That is where I drew the line.'
>
> 'My daughter is going to be our bridesmaid and I would like her grandparents from both sides to see her. My future wife is adamant that they can't come to the wedding. What can I do? Should I insist?'

This is another all-too-familiar e-mail message which comes my way through my website. I often feel that the question is really the tip of the iceberg, and that for this bridal couple there are still many unresolved issues. In fact, the query raises a whole host of questions in my mind. There is no 'right' answer to this dilemma, and it signals that there are matters that should be openly discussed if this family is to regroup into a new unit.

> '*I am getting married to a man who is divorced. I want to wear white and have the whole business. Is this okay?*'

I don't have a problem replying to the message of this e-mail which has a theme which comes up very often. If that is what the couple want, then why not? If this is a bride who accepts that her future husband has already been married, and she does, why should she not have the wedding she wants. Yet brides and grooms are still very wary of 'what people might think'.

Your new family and the wedding:

- You must tell your ex about the wedding before you tell the children.
- Tell the children together with your new partner about your decision.
- Give them time to 'digest' the news.
- Try to enlist the cooperation of the ex.
- Decide together whether you should meet up with the other parent.
- Ask the children how they would like to be included – and have some suggestions ready.
- Don't force a reluctant child to come to the ceremony.
- Don't give the other parent any extra work or financial outlay.
- Discuss the honeymoon. Is it for two, three, or even four?
- Remember, although this is your wedding day – you are 'marrying' a family.
- Try to select a gift they will treasure. Remember you are on your way to creating a bank of new family memories.
- Make certain that some of the wedding photographs show all the members of the new family together.
- Most important of all: don't dodge out of telling any children from a previous relationship that you are getting married, or remarried.

A wedding is a wedding and should be seen as a commitment and as the celebration of the loving union of two people. At every wedding the couple hope and pray that it will last a lifetime. Sadly, for many reasons, that is not always how it will turn out. You are older now, and wiser, than at the time of your first marriage and hopefully you are bringing to your new partnership the wisdom of your years and experience. With love in your heart, but with your feet on the ground, you will have banished the fantasy of a 'dream' lover, or an 'ideal' home. So, go for it, and have a lovely day and celebrate it in the way you want. This is a new chapter for the family, and every day you are helping to build a new platform to support you all. Hopefully your wedding day will be a day that memories are made of.

Stepparents have needs too

Right, the wedding is now a lovely memory and the honeymoon – with or without the children – is behind you. Real life is about to begin! Even if you have all been living together as a family for a while, the wedding will have made a difference to the family unit. You will probably feel you can relax a bit and that you are no longer on trial. (I believe it is hard for a step-to-be to feel otherwise.) But if you are about to start on the road towards making a new family, then there are some things to keep in mind.

The first thing I am going to mention may surprise you: it is that a stepparent has rights too. We have already looked at the right way to get to know the children, the problem of dealing with the other parent, measuring the impact on your own extended family, and looking after yourself. But now that you and your new husband – or wife – are the centre of the new family, you must recognize that private time for you as a couple is essential as well. You not only deserve this, but it is fundamental to the health of the family. The often mentioned 'quality time' isn't just for the kids, but for couples too. So make sure you build this into your schedule.

If one, or both of you, have been through the trauma of a broken romance you will know only too well that relationships need caring for, and this should not be lost sight of in the hurly-burly of family life. Especially a ready-made family. It is all too easy to let that happen. At the beginning of any important relationship everyone likes to keep things sweet, and to feel that they are in step. However, avoidance of conflict is no way to build a relationship. That can take you on the slippery slope which leads to not talking at all about important things, and we have already discussed where that can lead.

If you are a part-time stepparent, then the pressure will not be quite so great as if you have the children with you constantly. If they live with you, they may, or may not, spend time with their other parent. Either way this can be surprisingly disruptive, and a pattern and routine will need to be established. But do keep in mind that as you are beginning to make a new family, its own rituals, traditions and *rules* need to be established. It is a grave error to begin by compromising all the time. Of course there must be give and take, and I have been urging you to move cautiously, but there is a difference between feeling you have *no* say, and knowing that this is your home too.

Do it my way!

A problem can arise when you and your new partner have different standards of behaviour for children or views about hygiene or pocket money. But be careful of too many battles and remember the children may already be muddled by conflicting rules if they have two separate homes. Don't take anything for granted. Your way of looking at tidiness or time-keeping may be very different from what the children are used to, and they may take some time to fall into step, however willing they are.

Don't fall into the obvious trap of criticizing or blaming the other parent for something the children do or don't do. Instead, communicate in a tactful way how you like things done in your own home. Say this with some authority and, so long as there is mutual respect between you, you will find that the children should respond well. Maybe unwillingly and grudgingly at first, but hopefully this will settle down into an acceptable status quo, since kids do like to know where they stand. On the other hand, if, for example, a child is used to a particular routine at bedtime which is not familiar to you, learn from the child. And say so. That will be appreciated. Let them know you are up for new experiences too. Show them that change is not a thing to fear and that you, by example, are open to change. Don't expect them just to 'know' what you want. Just as *you* don't yet know their favourite food or TV programme or 'the best day' of their lives.

Discipline, you will already have discovered, is best left to the biological parent for a long, long time. Again, you may feel this is easier said than done, especially if the other parent is away from the home for any length of time, and you are the one holding the reins. If this is the case, then family conferences, and some agreement on basics, can ease the way.

Lizzie, a mother of three and a stepmother of two, told me of the greatest area of discord in her new family: the number of kids in the parents' bed!

> *'My children had never slept with me, but as soon as we all lived together, one, two and then more would creep into our bed at night.'*

She was astounded to see how quickly her own children joined in this nightly activity. Sex, she said, went right out of the window. In time, too, so did sleep. Lizzie told me that it was the first time a family conference was held, and to her surprise, it worked. She put her side of the story, the children put theirs, and the agreement was a huge family breakfast in bed on Saturdays and Sundays.

> *'Not ideal, but it seemed to fill a need the kids had to be right there with us. Actually it all fizzled out after a few weeks.'*

If you are leaving a great deal of the childcare to your new partner, have plenty of sympathy as he or she is in the hot seat and will need your support. It is no joke to be shouted at by a child, 'You are not my mum to tell me what to do' or, 'My dad would never make me eat that', when you know you are doing your best.

> 'You can't imagine the pain on Mother's Day when you think everything is going well, and your stepchild makes a card for her "real" mum, and nothing for you. Especially as Zoe's mum only sees her about once a year.'

The eleven-year-old who went happily on family outings with you before the marriage, may regress to behaviour more in keeping with a child half that age. See this for what it is: insecurity and anxiety caused by a world shifting again. An adolescent who answers you in monosyllabic tones, or blanks you out, may drive you to distraction. But remember, these are things we all did at times in our teens when we were uncertain or unsure. So try not to take these signs as something very wrong, but of a child unsure of finding his feet in this new world. Just because a boy or girl of fifteen or sixteen seems to want the world to treat them as an adult, it does not mean they can cope with it when it happens.

Don't greet your new spouse when he comes home at night with a list of complaints about the children. It is not helpful at the beginning of a marriage and you will not be thanked for making a parent piggy in the middle between you and the kids. No parent likes to be told that his child has been rude or misbehaved, and there is a chance it could turn into a row between the two of you! Take time to talk, as a couple and as a family. There may be sticking points with, for example, bedtimes. If your own children have been used to the routine of an early bedtime there may be ructions if you try to impose this timetable on your stepchildren. This is where you both, as parents, have to work out a compromise and show the kids that you are united with whatever scheme you come up with. Don't let yourself be pushed into agreeing to something which you know will enrage you. If, for instance, you like a child-free part of the evening, say so. Don't be put off by being told, 'But my mother lets me stay up' – this is your home and you won't be doing anyone any favours if you try to stretch yourself for another four or five hours every day. Some arbitration may mean you can adjust your ideas a little. Can you agree that at a certain hour the children can read or play in their bedrooms? Not lights out, but a time for them to be away from the grown-ups. Perhaps a concession from you about bedtimes at weekends will restore harmony.

Certainly don't let resentment build up in you to fever pitch. If there are things you are unhappy or uneasy about, don't ignore them. It may be mistaken for indifference or that you are uninvolved and not caring. So don't sit on the fence – it can hurt! It can be damaging, too, if you then feel misunderstood and it can harm the relationship if you do not make yourself and your opinions heard. It all comes down to valuing yourself, and if you don't do that, no one else will!

You are establishing new rituals for the children, while mindful of their earlier roots. Now is the time to begin a new family photo album, perhaps starting with the wedding photos we spoke about earlier. A thoughtful stepparent will also make sure that the children have a photo of their other parent, even if this is something you would rather not look at. Little things like that will help to make the children feel at home, even if they spend only some of their time with you. If they visit, make sure that if at all possible they do have some place they can call their own. Provide a corner where toothbrushes and nightware can be kept safe for each visit. It will make the transition easier if they don't have to bring everything with them each time. Even a locked box or drawer where they can store some of their precious belongings will be welcomed, and make them feel less like a 'visitor'. We all need some private space.

If at all possible arrange for them to have their own beds already made up, and looking inviting. Nothing is more guaranteed to make someone feel a stranger than waiting around while a bed is set up. Their arrival is a good time to establish new patterns of behaviour.

Perhaps sitting around the kitchen table, catching up on news while favourite snacks or drinks are consumed. Children love familiar routines. If your stepchildren come on visits, make sure they have some time to themselves too. It can be very tiring always to be on the move, and they will value your understanding about this. Also, know when to back off and leave them with their parent. They may have things to say to their mother or father that they are not ready yet to share with you.

If you have become a stepparent through the death of a parent be particularly sensitive to the grief the children may still be feeling. Don't blot out the memory of the parent or their earlier history. Keep in mind the important dates of anniversaries and birthdays when a child may feel especially low and bereft. This will apply too if their other parent is still alive, but for one reason or another, is not in touch. Even if you feel that the other parent has misbehaved or acted in a cruel or callous way, be careful what you say. Against all the odds, a missing biological parent still has a place in a child's heart.

Checklist for the new stepparent:

- Are you remembering you have rights too?
- Are you speaking with authority?
- Do you remember respect is a two-way street?
- Are you watching out for the new couple, as well as the family?
- Are you beginning to introduce new rituals and customs around celebrations and visits?
- Do you agree – or compromise – on house rules?
- Are you learning from the children too?
- Do you hold back on criticizing the children to their parent? If you have a problem, sort it out!
- Do you leave the discipline, on the whole, but make clear what you expect from them?
- Are you making sure visiting stepchildren are felt welcome on arrival?

- Are you giving them some privacy and time alone with their parent?
- Are you keeping your sense of humour?

More yes's than no's? You are on your way alright.

Blended families

A 'blended family' is one which comes into being when both parents have a child or children from a previous relationship. And in these circumstances creating a new family needs extra skills. Sixty-five per cent of remarriages now include such parents, so the number of blended families is increasing all the time. We are now all familiar with the idea of 'one parent' families and 'single parent' families and even 'stepfamilies', but 'blended families' and the extra pressures upon them are not so quickly acknowledged.

Although you and your new love may have whispered together in an excited way about how the kids will get on, and even had a shared fantasy that they would quickly merge into a loving group, it may not turn out to be so simple. You may both have thought that for an only child to suddenly find a new ready-made brother and sister would make him feel he was in heaven. Well, yes and no. The reality will need working on. You may already have met up with both sets of children, and watched carefully as they eyed each other. There may even have been a honeymoon period with shared outings which have been enjoyed by children and parents alike.

Don't take anything for granted. Just because you both have eight-year-olds, you cannot assume that they will hit it off and be best friends. They may like to play together, cautiously, at first. But once there is the idea of a wedding in the air, this may alter. The very thought that 'my' mother or 'my' father will also become 'your' mother or 'your' father, may bring tension into the relationship. But hopefully not, and if the kids have begun to feel easier with each

154

other and if you both, as parents, have kept a careful watch on things, how will it go from here? First reassure – and reassure again – that becoming a new mother or father is the last thing on anyone's mind, and you do not plan to step into anyone else's shoes.

Remember that the children will already have been through the trauma of the break-up of a family, from whatever cause, and then had to adjust to living with one parent, while perhaps visiting the other parent. So it will be another hurdle to overcome to even think of becoming part of a new composite family and to have to *share* with another child or children. Consider the changes that there may be. The eldest may no longer be the eldest, or the youngest no longer the baby of the family. An only child may suddenly be one of five! But take heart, not all these changes are negative. Think of the extra experiences your child will have. Think of the extra loving people who will be around throughout their lives. But at the beginning bedrooms may have to be shared, so will videos, computers *and* mother or father. And that takes time to accept.

Sharing and caring

First of all, where will you be living? Circumstances may dictate that it is just not possible for you all to have a brand new home to start off in. It can be quite difficult if one of you moves with your children into the home already occupied by a single parent with his or her children, since this will inevitably mean much moving over and sharing. Add to that the possibility that the children of the first family may remember their now non-resident parent living there, and the sparks can fly.

It is never easy to see a new mum in the kitchen, or a new dad mowing the lawn using Dad's lawnmower, but much will depend on how old the children are, and how and why the first family broke up. If there has been a death in the family, and there has been sufficient time for grief and mourning, it may well be a great comfort for the children to see they are a complete family again. Be careful about being too quick to change things around. Of course you will want to reorganize things and make the home your own. But it can be less obvious and upsetting if you add new things at first, rather than getting rid of things in the home which, unknown to you, may have memories attached to them.

Coming and going

Perhaps one of the most difficult periods is when you are trying to be a blended family and the children go off to stay with the other parent.

> *Just as we got settled Holly would go to her dad. We didn't know whether to still do nice things without her with tears from Holly on her return. Or just to hang around with tears from my two.'*

This is the kind of dilemma which a blended family will come up against. It can be very unsettling trying to incorporate the plans of so many people. It is hard enough if there is agreement, and everyone keeps to the schedule, but if there is an unreliable parent, or an ill or fractious child, any plans made can fly out of the window at the last moment. Any holiday plans will have to be made weeks in advance. Don't assume that the children will necessarily be with you; on the other hand don't assume either that you will have a childfree time! If you are planning for a big family holiday remember to consider the views of the other parents, grandparents, siblings and anyone else who would like to have a say in the arrangements and may have plans too. Remember, though, you can only do what you can do. Nowhere is the saying 'You can't please all of the people all of the time' more apt than in a blended family: this is a mantra which many a mother mutters to herself under her breath when trying to hold everything together and to organize events.

A local blended family I know told me that each year it seemed that they could never be all together to celebrate Christmas Day. So they decided on a date which they designated as the Brown's Family Day. This was a date they celebrated each year and looked forward to. It became part of their ritual and their family history.

As the children grew up and left home, they would all move heaven and earth to be back together for that day. Nowadays, some of the children bring *their* children home too to celebrate the Brown's Family Day. A lovely tradition.

Watch out for the children keeping an eye on you and everything that is going on. They will be doing just that. They will be looking to see who gets the largest piece of pie and the biggest share of your attention. The greatest danger at this time is to over-compensate in favour of your stepchildren. You may think your children already know you love them and they will be able to let you be more generous to your new stepchildren. They won't. Keep in mind that your children are dealing with change too, and will probably need *more* reassurance from you that you love them. There are many bewildered stepparents feeling that although they bend over backwards to 'be fair' to their stepchildren, they are then accused of unfairness by their own child or children.

Don't feel consumed by guilt if you know that you love your children more than your stepchildren. How could it be otherwise? You and your own children have had time to grow and to bond together – so give yourself and your stepchildren time to forge new links. Don't fool yourself and try to believe you love them all the same. Even if you like to think you do, the children will know otherwise.

Am I being fair?

Danger ahead when there are gifts to be chosen!

> 'His kids get presents from us and their mother and grandparents and uncles and aunts. My kids only get gifts from us. Should I give them more than my stepchildren?'

First of all, agree as parents what your policy is. Finance may well be a consideration here. One way that a family I know dealt with this was to give the same number of gifts at Christmas and Thanksgiving (remember the children will be sizing up each other's piles) and to give each child on their birthday something special. For example, when one set of grandparents gave their two grandchildren bicycles for Christmas, Joe and Jenny bought the other children bikes for their birthdays. Smiles all round.

One more thing, I'm afraid. Do try to give each child a little time with you on his or her own even if it is a quick trip to the supermarket, or making the beds together. With time at a premium you may discover that just chatting at bath time is another way. This is a good method of keeping in touch with the little things which can worry children. You may notice something which is not so visible when you are all together as a family. You may be able to smooth out a misunderstanding which if undetected would have rapidly grown into a real problem. You may want to hold your head in your hands with despair as you try to find time to merge them all together; there are occasions when you are sure to feel you are running out of time and energy.

> '*I felt as if I was made of velcro. Overnight my children, who had become pretty self-sufficient, suddenly "forgot" how to do things that they had been doing for years. They literally stuck to my sides. I just didn't have enough lap for five.*'

If you are now dividing your time between twice as many children, and a new partner, something will have to give. It might be high standards in the house, or entertaining, or work outside the home, but it will be a time when you will both have to plough a great deal into the family. A daunting statistic is that more second marriages with children break up than first marriages. So take care.

Yours, mine, and . . . ours?

Are you considering whether to have a baby of your own now? Even hoping that the arrival of a new baby may help to cement you all together? Can you cope? Is it the time? I think that a baby can sometimes put as much strain on a relationship as an affair, so let the family settle first. At the right time, a new baby does seem to do the trick. This may be affected by the ages of the children already in the family. Are they able to take another change? Tread carefully. Take heed that it will mean everyone has to shift their position in the family again. It can be a wonderful moment for a blended family when you can all celebrate 'our' baby.

It can certainly be a blow if one of the children decides they want to change the arrangements and go to live with the other parent. Don't see this, or any other family row, as 'the end'. *All* families have disagreements at times. It is how these misunderstandings are resolved which is important. Although it may disrupt the family pattern you have been trying to create, an adolescent may want to spread his wings as a way of asserting his independence and so he says he wants to leave the family. Take a look and try to see if it is a reaction to the marriage, or whether you both believe this would have happened in any case. The kindest thing you can do is to accept that your stepchild may want to belong to two families. Either way, it should not be taken automatically as a criticism of you and your partner and the other children.

> *'When Pam said she wanted to go and live with her mum my husband turned to me and asked what I had said to her. We had the first of many huge rows.'*

There may be times when you long to speak to another stepparent. To learn from others who have successfully blended together children from earlier relationships. If so, look at Chapter Nine for some resources. There are plenty at hand, and mutual support will help you to keep afloat if you are in danger of drowning. BUT remember that each of the issues you face each day are a step (I can't help feeling this pun has a special relevance) to becoming a successful stepparent. You will meet many challenges on the way. Each time you slay dragons whose names are jealousy, resentment, rivalry, grief, or misunderstanding, your children, your stepchildren and your new partner will love you for it.

Yet another divorce

Sadly, there are step- and blended families who don't make it. The stress is just too much. If two families have joined up too quickly, or there are too many memories or ghosts around, then even the most dedicated parents finds that they have to call it a day.

'I have two very small children and thought taking on two adolescents as well would be okay. But within weeks I was in over my head with decisions about drugs, all-night parties and sex. We struggled on for two years, and then I had to pull out.'

'We would have been alright as a family. What was too much was that my son saw his dad very irregularly, his son saw his dad three times a week. It was a case of too little and too much. The kids couldn't take it, and in the end neither could we. The strain of it all made me very ill. My miscarriage was the last straw.'

'To my shame it was having a stepson who was very disabled which actually broke our marriage. I willingly took on a handicapped little boy, but it all got too much. His mother faded out of the picture completely. The "baby" I was left to hold was too heavy.'

'I realized too late that my new husband had looked for a mother for his kids, not a wife. I knew within a week it wouldn't work. The children never took to me.'

None of those who spoke to me said they had fallen out of love with their partners, just that family life got too much. Was the reason for the break-up because the other parent was not around enough of the time when all this was going on? As I said earlier, if you are not the parent with the day-to-day hands-on childcare do make sure you play your part in parenting. Don't assume that your partner who may be a whiz at looking after one or two young children will be equally equipped to manage your children too, when this may mean coping with four or five children of different ages from day one.

Is it possible to imagine in advance just how hard it is to organize the comings and goings of children? The problem is that when a couple fall in love they feel they can cope with anything the world throws at them. We all do it. Your children? My children? Ex-partners? Of course we can! We love each other. Yes, but time and again we learn that love is not enough. In order to survive, a family needs love, certainly, but also cooperation and a genuine desire to merge and to pull together.

> 'You can have no idea how awful it is to hear your own children at loggerheads with their stepfather. I know what it is like to be torn in two.'

Goodness knows it is hard enough to be a mother or father in happy circumstances. Add to the pot worries about financing more than one family, anxiety about your child living a thousand miles away, an un-cooperative ex, no sign of a let-up in the ongoing battles between the children of the blended family, and no wonder some parents buckle under the strain.

Get as much help as you can. Don't wait until the family reaches crisis point. What you may be putting down to teething troubles could actually be the sign of something much more serious. Rope in the grandparents to give you a weekend off. Talk to other parents, try to engage the children to be as cooperative as they can be. Get some professional help either for yourself or for the children if you believe that their behaviour is still a sign that they have been affected by all the changes.

> *'I wouldn't have believed what a difference it would make to talk to another stepfamily. Thank God for the Internet. I learnt to laugh off some of the things which had made me weep.'*

The splitting up of any family is heartbreaking but for it to happen a second time is totally shattering. Even if all the pros and cons have been evaluated before setting up home together, it is almost impossible to know what the chemistry will be like until there is the regular hurly-burly of family life. All too often, although both parents try their best, the children may have other ideas, and it is not beyond them to sabotage a relationship. That is why I have tried to spell out all the possible danger areas. And to provide early warnings.

A second marriage will not have been entered into lightly, and neither will a subsequent divorce. Especially when there is, once again, the effect on the children to consider. Knowing that for them as well as yourself – and everyone else involved – you are going to cover all-too-familiar ground has probably already made your blood run cold.

> *'My second divorce was worse, much worse, than the first. The children were devastated, and my stepson was distraught. I hoped to keep in touch with Pete, but my ex thought otherwise. But his drinking was too much and I had to go. I went through agony, but there was no other way.'*
>
> *'No way could I stay there with my children. I tried, I really tried. But she really was a cruel stepmother and that is no joke. Her children could do no wrong, but mine suffered a lot.'*

So hearts get broken once again. You may be asking yourself how could this have happened to you? Even if you have tried to follow through with being understanding and considerate you have to accept that other people may be driven by motives which are totally different from yours. A stepparent trying from day one to be honest, fair and caring will not succeed if the odds are stacked against him from the start. If an earlier relationship has not truly been cleared up, and if the emotional ties have not been broken with an earlier partner, then these unseen and unconscious factors will also be present. Sometimes they are not really concealed.

> 'His ex was so demanding. Even after we were married she would ring about every little emergency. I was furious that he would go and sort her out and leave me with all the kids here. He went on giving her money we couldn't afford. I think he still felt guilty, I can't believe he did it from love.'

Because of the children you still have contact with the other parent and confusion can spill over into the new family. Childcare arrangements which may have been tolerated when you were a single parent can put a terrible strain on a stepfamily. Any new couple settling into married life has to find the way to a meeting ground. But with two, three or more squabbling children who are dead set against the whole idea of a stepfamily, the sparks will fly. You may have discovered that by holding back your anger towards your step-children, it bursts out towards your own kids or your new partner. That is what Adam found.

> 'I would hear them all yelling and I was scared of being the heavy with my stepkids. That meant I would have a go at my boys, which of course they thought was unfair. That would ignite the whole issue, and when my new wife jumped in, it became a free-for-all. I loved Annie very much, but Annie plus her kids, plus my kids and my ex – well, who could have managed that and been able to smile.'

All the research into successful stepfamilies shows that it takes several years for a stepfamily to settle down. So if you are about to embark with a new love into a stepfamily or blended family, hold on tight. You are in for a rollercoaster of a ride.

You are taking things for granted if you assume that:

- The children will merge together happily without your intervention.
- The children will not mind that they have to share their mum or dad.
- Sharing a room, TV programme, pets or parents will just happen.
- You can make changes in the furnishings or decoration in the home as soon as you like.
- The children will be with you for the holidays.
- The children will not be with you for the holidays.
- The other parent or relatives will not have different opinions about the holidays.
- You will love all the children equally.
- You will buy gifts without a struggle about 'being fair'.
- You will have plenty of time to be alone with each child.
- You will find it easy to decide when to have 'our' baby.
- You will not be affected if a child wants to leave and live with the other parent.
- You don't need any help and have not set up a support group or contact.
- You will never divorce.

Single parenting

We have already considered some strategies for caring for yourself again as a 'single'. It is, however, much more difficult to do this when you are a parent. After the break-up of a family you will, unless you are living with a new partner, find yourself as a single

164

parent. Whether you have sole care, shared care, occasional care or break off all contact with your child, you have now joined the ever-growing ranks of lone parents. To be a single parent brings with it very mixed experiences and feelings.

Perhaps you are wondering what it will be like to bring up the children by yourself. If you and your ex have never agreed on childcare anyway, you may have a feeling of well-being knowing that you won't have to fight over every single family issue.

> *'I didn't think it would be any different. Ben was away so much that I felt like a single parent anyway. Actually, I was wrong. I hadn't bargained on the fact that I did feel backed up by Ben, even if he wasn't there. And I could, at times, say to the kids, "No, your father and I have said you can't". It gave me more authority I suppose.'*

But although you might rub your hands with glee at the thought that you will be the one holding the reins now over matters such as discipline and pocket money, the everyday responsibilities will weigh heavily at times. It is no joke to be the one who always has to say 'no' when impossible plans are put up for approval. If there are loving grandparents on the scene, ask for their cooperation. Tell them what a struggle it is for you at times. It certainly won't help if they continue to be the doting grandparents when asked if bedtime can be extended and if they are heard to say, 'Oh let them, just this once,' about something you have vetoed.

It can stretch a single parent to breaking point to have the total responsibility for being at school events, and fetching and carrying children – often in different directions at the same time. Try to get into as many shared journeys as you can, although that in itself can sometimes bring on feelings of stress when it is your turn and you have a car load of kids to deliver. When one child is sick and you are housebound, everyday commitments become a nightmare. Don't lie awake at night fretting about how you are going to get the others to school in the morning. As something like this is certain to happen sooner or later, make sure you have a contingency plan. You will find that people are willing to help, so be sure you get into some give-and-take relationships and that there are some others mums who know they can ring you too in an emergency.

Don't let too many jobs pile up until an essential one becomes one difficult job too many. For example, if you can afford it, try to get someone to cut the grass for you. There may be a young lad in the neighbourhood who will be pleased to earn some pocket money. Don't let it grow knee high while you are waiting for your ex to come and deal with it. Every time you look out of the window you will feel your temperature rise. Keep your strength and energy for the things you have to do. As the kids get older and stronger they can help out in more ways too.

> 'I didn't cry about him leaving us until one day I found I just couldn't open a cupboard door. Silly, but I just sat on the floor and wept for a long long time. Even after that it was always when I was hopeless at a physical task that I felt most vulnerable.'

Many men and women who have talked to me about making the transition from a couple to being a lone parent, found the difficulties arose when the children got older and began to push against the boundaries, as adolescents feel they must do.

> 'It was fine when I just got on looking after my seven- and nine-year-olds. But I wasn't ready five years later when all kinds of things had to be decided. What time is it reasonable for them to come home? What is the proper bedtime for a fourteen-year-old? Is it okay for them to sleep over at a home where I don't know the parents?'

These are decisions which can be a real burden for a single mother or father when there is nobody to talk them over with. You may feel that however supportive the grandparents are to you and the children, times change, and so their measuring stick about what is okay and what is unacceptable, is no longer relevant today. Neither can you fully trust your children to tell you what their friends really are allowed to do. Don't you remember telling your parents that 'everybody' had the latest fashions, and that 'everybody' was allowed to stay up really, *really* late even on a school night? Yes, now you remember. So be cautious about believing everything you are told.

If you are involved with shared care, which we looked at in Chapter Five, or even if the other parent has limited access, you will want to try to engage him or her in some of the decisions. The trouble may arise if the parent with more hands-on care sees things one way, and the other parent takes a more relaxed view and opts for a quiet life by saying 'okay'.

> *'Relaxed view? I see my ex taking irresponsible views all the time. I don't call that relaxed.'*

A parent who sees a child infrequently may be wary of becoming the strict parent in case the child will not want to visit. In the same way there are many parents with the lion's share of caring for their kids who are equally fearful of setting too many boundaries in case the child decides to go and live with the other parent. This may result in a most unhappy double bind for the children, who are not sure where the limits lie, and may manipulate the situation to their own advantage. This difference of opinion about what is permitted and what is not can often drive a final wedge between two people who hoped to continue to share parenting, even though they could not go on living together. 'I am not divorcing my children' has quite a ring about it. But what does it mean in practice?

When Bob left Ruth these were the words he used. He took them to mean that he could see his children when and where he liked. Ruth, believing quite rightly that children need both parents, tried to fit in with his erratic plans. What she found in reality was that she became the one who had most care of the children, while Bob popped in whenever he felt like it, often staying on to watch TV and to have supper. Ruth was in despair as she felt she had no private life but didn't want to prevent the children seeing their father. Once she found her feet she tried to stop Bob from coming to see his sons without making an arrangement in advance. Bob was outraged at this and threatened to stop seeing them altogether. Ruth backtracked and things went on as before. Does this seem a familiar scenario to you? Not being married and yet not being single either. Friends criticized Ruth for 'putting up' with these arrangements but she felt she had to put the boys first even at great inconvenience to herself. She was also fearful that Bob would cut back on the financial arrangement he had agreed. It was only when Ruth met someone she wanted to start dating that she felt able to tell Bob the visits with the children had to be put on a regular footing and that she needed time for herself. Much to her surprise, Bob agreed and even seemed happy to take them off to his new home and partner.

This story is an example of the different ways parents manage (or don't manage) the transition from being a family to becoming single parents. It was two years later that Bob told Ruth he was too scared to take the boys on his own at the beginning. He said that he had felt so bad at leaving them all, that he could only cope by coming back home as often as he could. Bob also confessed he had been wary of asking Ruth if the boys could meet his new partner. How sad that they did not sort this out from the start. There had been many tears along the way before this family settled down into a more comfortable routine.

Barry, who has sole care of his two daughters, found the first really difficult hurdle was when another parent wouldn't let her twelve-year-old daughter sleep over one night because there was no woman in the house.

'I was so taken aback I couldn't answer. What did she think I was going to do? The girls had played together for years.'

If you are about to be a single parent, and you have young children, think ahead to when you will be dealing with much older children who have a different set of concerns. A single mother might quake at the thought of five fifteen-year-old boys watching a match and sharing a pizza.

'What if they want beer? If so, how much is okay? Oh, God, will they want to sleep over?'

Being a single parent at school functions can be hard and at the beginning, you may feel you are the only one not in a couple. But these days you can be sure that you won't be the only single parent at the sports day or concert. So it should be possible to link up with another parent or group of parents.

'The thing I hated most about being a single parent was when dealing with a mechanic or someone fixing a machine. I actually found myself saying "My husband this" and "My husband that", because you really do need a man's voice when you are complaining. I hated doing it, but learnt it was the only way.'

Today the words 'single parent' or 'lone parent' still carry with them a picture often painted in gloomy colours by the media and by politicians. You may find you become an easy target for criticism. It is not encouraging if almost every time you pick up a newspaper you are told how studies show that children thrive best with two parents who are married and living together. As you struggle over daily worries, comments in the press really do rub salt into the wound. It is as well to keep in mind that there are difficulties for all parents coping with the workaday life of bringing up a family. You know that, and I know that. But it doesn't read so well in the press! Unfortunately every time more statistics are published about under-age pregnancies, drinking or drugs, the finger is pointed at children from broken homes.

Too often people who don't know you, or your circumstances, will make their minds up unfairly about you and your children. You will find that everybody has an opinion about divorce and its effect upon children. The very last thing you will want to hear are stories about 'other people's' divorces, problems with child-care or worse still, abduction and alienation of affection. You will find you are on the receiving end of horror stories that make your hair curl, and your assurance that you and the kids are doing okay will often be met with disbelief.

Apart from your children

If your children do not live with you, you will find that you become the object of questions and curiosity once people begin to ask you about them. How are you to reply when asked if you have children? If you say 'yes' there will be the inevitable follow-on questions, some of which you may not be able to answer. People, often total strangers, feel they have the right to ask the most intrusive questions.

> *'I met this woman at a party and when I told her I was getting a divorce she raged off at me about till death do us part. She didn't wait for me to say it was my husband who had left me with two-year-old twins.'*

If you are not in touch with your children at all it will be especially painful, but to say, 'Yes, I do have children, but do not see them,' will unleash a barrage of questions. On the other hand, to hear yourself say you do not have any children, so as to spare yourself the probing, can be the most painful cut of all.

The silent home

It can be unbelievably lonely when the children go out for the day, or begin to stay with the other parent. Although you may look forward to some respite, it often doesn't seem like that. But do try to use the time to please yourself. Don't spend this free period clearing out their rooms, or fretting about what they are all doing without you. Take the day off, in every sense of the word. You will feel better for it, and the children will come home to a refreshed and relaxed mother or father. Take the time to unwind. If the children are still very young and only go for a couple of hours, have a long soak in the bath or even a nap. If they are away for longer, think in advance how you will spend your leisure. Of course the house will seem very silent, but fill it with music you like for once, or the chatter of some friends or family.

> 'I used to mope around, feeling resentful that they were off having a good time with their dad and his new girlfriend, whilst I was left to feed the rabbit, the guinea pigs and the cat. I was crabby when they came home and I know I spoilt their day for them.'

Tips for being a single parent:

- Make sure you have a close friend, preferably another single parent, to compare notes with.
- If at all possible, try to make some of the day-to-day decisions about the children with your ex.
- Grandparents aren't always the best people to ask about boundaries to set for the kids. Times change!

- But grandparents can be very helpful with the ferrying around and babysitting.
- Don't believe all that your children tell you about what their peers are allowed to do.
- Don't feel you have to disclose your feelings about being a single parent to everyone who asks.
- Chat to other single parents on-line, and share some of the day to day worries with them too.
- Don't put your life on hold when the children are with their other parent.

Part Three

Help is at Hand

The voice of the intellect is a soft one, but it does not rest till it has gained a hearing.
(Sigmund Freud)

8

The 'Talking Cures'

A merry heart maketh a cheerful countenance:
but by sorrow of the heart the spirit is broken.
(Proverbs 15:13)

Do I need to talk to a professional?

If this thought has crossed your mind you probably followed it with a number of questions, such as, 'How would I know?', 'Would it help me?', 'What kind of help should I look for?', 'Where would I find someone I can trust?' and 'How much will it cost me?' On the other hand maybe professional help is not something you want to consider at the moment, especially if you are surrounded and comforted by caring family or friends. You may find that you are too occupied with day-to-day practical issues to consider thinking about your own mental health. But keep in mind that there are people trained to help you if you want to take that road.

> *'I wish I had gone to see a counsellor when my marriage broke up, it was only much later I realized what a terrible effect it had all had on me. I wasted a couple of years and I regret that.'*

Don't fall into the trap of thinking that because you know other people who have been through a divorce and they seem okay, you should battle through on your own. You may not know about the tears when they are alone, or the loss of self-esteem which affects them so painfully.

There are times when well-intentioned friends or loving family just will not do. One of the reasons for this is that those who love us want us to feel better *now*, and it makes them happier if they can come up with a practical suggestion which you can agree to. If you are struggling with very black and painful feelings it won't actually help if it is suggested you 'get your hair cut in a new style' or if you are offered a meal out as a 'treat'. It can be hard to refuse these well-meaning friends, and it can hurt when they steer the conversation away from what you really want and need to talk endlessly about.

The idea of seeing a counsellor – a professional trained to listen and to help in a special way – is gradually becoming acceptable to more and more people. No longer is it necessary to keep painful thoughts and feelings to ourselves. It is no longer seen as stoic to 'suffer' quietly on your own.

> *'I never ever thought I would see a counsellor. Yet when my husband told me he had had an affair for three years my first thought was, "Oh my God, perhaps I have AIDS". I could never have told my family or friends of my fear, so I reached for the telephone for help and it truly saved my life.'*

Fortunately, every situation now seems to be covered by a helpline, often with the opportunity to speak with a counsellor. Helplines are usually manned by volunteers who give their time to help others going through the same crises they once went through themselves. You will find them understanding and competent to give you information about local services or resources.

In today's climate some companies have learnt to their advantage that if they employ a staff counsellor the efficiency of their employees increases and absences due to stress-related illness are reduced. So too is conflict amongst the staff. So if you work for a large company, does your employer offer this service? If you are a student, find out about counselling facilities at your college or university.

If there is a rail crash or a fire or any other major incident, both the victims and the many people attached to the support services who come to their aid are more often than not offered the help of a counsellor. What, then, if there is a major *emotional* incident like a divorce? Should you consider approaching the 'right' kind of professional to guide you through the aftermath of a break-up?

How would I know?

In everyone's life there are highs and lows and there will be times when all of us feel more vulnerable than usual. Recovering from a family break-up is often one of those times. It is when the feelings of deep depression or crippling anxiety seem to be getting out of proportion and affecting your daily life that you need to consider professional help. If you feel that life is not worth living, if you have prolonged sleep disturbance, bouts of crying or if you are over-whelmed by feelings of hopelessness or despair, to an extent way beyond your situation, then you should look for help.

> *'I thought it would be better to go and see someone to talk about the break-up. I felt it was either that or a breakdown.'*

> *'I had to talk to someone. I thought I was going to go mad deciding whether to leave my husband. What was best for the children – to be with a man who was mentally ill so much of the time, or for them to be without a dad altogether? I just went round and round in my mind.'*

Be on the alert for physical symptoms such as excessive tiredness or headaches which may indicate that something is psychologically wrong. There is a strong link between mind and body, and we often give confused signals even to ourselves. We need to learn to decode these messages. Try asking yourself if it is easier to say, 'I'm not well' rather than 'I'm depressed'.

What can I expect?

No counsellor can help you to put back together your 'old' world and life. To look for help believing that is possible will lead you to a dead-end and more disappointment. You may find, as many men and women who are facing a broken relationship do, that you need to talk about it all and that you are searching for answers about *why* the relationship went wrong. No friend, however loving, is qualified to give you the kind of satisfactory answer you are seeking. And this is where a trained counsellor can help.

> *'What I wanted to hear was an explanation. Something I could UNDERSTAND. I felt so confused. Three years on I still don't know why she left me for someone else.'*
>
> *'I decided it was time to see a counsellor when I found myself looking for excuses to keep my twelve-year-old up at night so that I could talk about what had happened, and what I was scared of happening.'*

'My ex-husband and I were divorced ten years ago. The next eight years passed in a kind of blur. Eventually I saw a therapist, and it was hard work getting emotionally divorced. But I got there. What a lot of time I wasted.'

Even during this time of stress it is important to keep in mind that family and friends do have their own lives to live, and a neighbour or colleague who was willing to be at the end of a phone for you twenty-four hours a day, may in time begin to wilt. If you feel this may be about to happen to you, then now is the time to think of seeing a counsellor. Someone who will offer you support and who will help you to get clearer in your own mind some of the thoughts which may be racing round and keeping you awake at night. Someone to help you get out of the endless loop of confusion and turmoil.

One of the benefits of seeing a counsellor is that he or she will be someone who has no contact with the rest of your life and they will not have any personal reason for 'taking sides' or having a biassed point of view. There is relief in knowing that the person you are talking to is there specifically to listen to you, and that you have a regular time to meet which is yours to use in the way that is most helpful to you.

Help on the world wide web

The Internet is no substitute for individual counselling but it has opened doors for many people. There have always been 'agony' columns in newspapers and magazines, where everyday questions can be discussed and advice given, but today you can post a message on an Internet site and sometimes get replies in minutes. This can be a good starting point before you decide to take the final step of finding a therapist or counsellor.

To 'talk' to other people who have been, or are in, the same boat as you can feel like a lifesaver and may help to keep you afloat. For example, if you are a mother separated from your children you will find great support and advice from MATCH (Mothers Apart from their Children). This is a support network run by volunteers who are, or have been, mothers separated from their children in a variety of circumstances. They will empathize with you and understand that to be without your children can feel like a never-ending bereavement. There are members from across the world and of all ages. You will find MATCH is entirely non-judgmental and supportive of all mothers. Visit their website (www.match1979.co.uk) or write to them at MATCH c/o BM Problems London WC1N 3XX, and please do send a stamped addressed envelope for a reply.

Whereas you may feel you have to keep up a pretence when you are with a friend, it is less inhibiting to e-mail some faceless person over 3,000 miles away who is wrestling with the same problem. My own website (www.familyonwards.com) has flourished in a way I could never have believed. At first I published a number of articles about different family issues on the site and invited anyone to e-mail me with comments or questions. I had no idea how familyonwards would be received, or even if there was a need for it. I soon discovered that there was! The e-mails I receive each day often end with words such as, 'Sorry to go on like this, but there is nobody else to tell' or, 'Please help me – I don't know who else to turn to'. I also get replies thanking me for 'listening', for taking the time to read about someone's situation, and for 'allowing them the space to vent'. There are a lot of lonely, frightened people around and for them the web can often be invaluable.

Of course, e-mail is not a substitute for counselling and it should not be taken as such, but many men and women appreciate being able to click on to a helpful and supportive network.

When Paul Maitland went through a divorce he chose the Internet as his sounding board and in his spare time he created a website (www.ondivorce.co.uk). He doesn't pretend to be an expert, but points people in the direction of organizations which can help. He also provides a forum for people with similar experiences to communicate with each other. He now provides the kind of support for others that he would have liked to have found when he was in the middle of the break-up of his family. Take a look at www.separation.org.uk which is a fairly new site with much to recommend it. Check out their news section for up-to-the-minute articles about people and the law. You will also find many of your questions answered in their reference section.

The Children's Rights Council at www.info4parents.com. is an American non-profit organization which offers help to parents, regardless of their marital status, who want to keep contact with their children. For anyone going through a divorce, or separation, and looking for help with his or her succeeding lifestyle there is www.uniqueyou.co.uk. It is a well put together site, bursting with up-to-date information that can help you through different stages of break-up and recovery. For women, www.everywoman.co.uk covers both professional and family life, with 'experts' at hand to answer your questions. Another friendly site well worth visiting is www.women.com. If you need some support about abuse in your relationship look at www.brokenspirits.com.

There are many websites on the net for parents. Not only are there sites if you want to chat to people *before* you have a baby (take a look at www.babyennouncements.com), but if you need help or advice on a child with special needs visit www.sickchildren.org.uk. If you have a child with a disability or illness get all the information you can to help you make informed choices. Seek out www.healthcentre.org.uk for information too. If your child has chronic fatigue syndrome (ME) or cancer there are specific sites with much information, and support for you too. The sites for children and teenagers with cancer or leukaemia, www.teencancer.org and www.youngactiononline.com for young sufferers of ME, are especially lively and helpful.

I can't list all the wonderful helplines there are for specific illnesses or disabilities, but they are there so search for them. A good starting point is www.adviceguide.org.uk. An excellent general parenting site is www.ukparents.co.uk. This is a site run by parents, for parents. There are chat boards on a huge variety of topics, and much more. One of the most helpful and lively sites for parents of children up to the age of seven (www.practicalparent.org.uk), is under the guidance of Dr Andy Gill, a psychologist. This site also has a very useful message board where parents can ask for help over specific worries and in return other parents share their experiences. There is nothing so reassuring as knowing you are not the only one wrestling with a predicament.

If you are a stepparent and want help, then visit www.stepfamilies.co.uk and talk to other stepparents. In the US there is www.saafamilies.org (or telephone 1-800-735-0329) for the Stepfamily Association of America. Do visit Stepmother International at www.stepmothers.org (although fathers and stepchildren are welcome too). Their aim is to create a worldwide organization and network of stepfamilies. Meanwhile, there is plenty of good educational material and support on their site. See also www.stepfamilyinfo.org, www.stepcarefully.com and www.Sfhelp.org. For blended families visit www.familyfusion.com 'where blended families come together'. There is no need to feel you are the only one!

Are you a second wife? Get some support from www.secondwives club.com. A lone parent? Visit www.planetoneparent.com where you will be almost overwhelmed by the helpful information available. In Singapore a new site, www.moms4moms.org, is a helpful place for mothers to visit. These sites are just the tip of the iceberg of the help available. All of them are interesting and there are places to have a laugh too; not all of them, by any means, are full of woe!

If you don't have access to the Internet then Parentline is a national telephone helpline for anyone in a parenting role: (telephone: 0808 800 2222). If their line is busy keep trying. They offer help and information to over eighty-five thousand families each year. They also have a website, www.parentlineplus.org.uk. It may be that this kind of support is enough for you at this time. However, if this is not the case, you may have already decided you want to look for more individual help.

Other useful helplines

If you are feeling anxious, depressed or experiencing total despair what should you do? For an emergency in the UK the Samaritans immediately comes to mind. There is always someone on the end of the telephone to listen to your cries (see telephone book for local numbers). The increased number of calls they receive each year indicates the desperate need so many of us have to talk to someone who will listen. Their latest innovation is an e-mail service (visit their website on www.samaritans.org) and many people seem to prefer this way of communicating. Whether you telephone or contact them by e-mail you will receive non-judgmental support.

If you are a woman and need help in a crisis there is the Women's Aid National Helpline on 08457 023468, their website at www.womensaid.org.uk or e-mail at wafe@wafe.co.uk. They can be a veritable port in a storm, as many women testify. In the last year for which figures are available over 22,000 women called their Domestic Violence Helpline. If you – or someone you know – is being abused get a copy of their booklet; this provides all the constructive information you need. It also contains some important advice about making a crisis safety plan, recommending that you make sure you know how to contact an emergency number at any time and advising you to set up an arrangement with a neighbour if you are not able to use the telephone. Don't be afraid to contact Women's Aid; they appreciate that freeing yourself from abuse can be a lengthy process. Many women leave and return a number of times before they can finally make the break. Remember that domestic violence is rarely a one-off event, so talk to them.

Keep in mind that there are many local Women's Aid groups who will also provide outreach support to women who may or may not want or need a refuge but who do need advice and support. And if you do need to seek refuge, they will help you find a place where you can get a safe breathing space and make decisions free from fear. There are also specialist refuges and services for women and children who face the additional pressures of racism or who have specific cultural needs. Have a look at www.domesticviolencedata.org which is a goldmine of information about domestic abuse in the UK. It also has a list of resources which offer immediate help and sanctuary. If there is abuse in your life, don't wait another moment to find practical help.

Although I am mainly referring to the help which is available for women, keep in mind that men are victims of violence too. Erin Pizzey, who founded the first refuge for battered women and children in Chiswick in 1971, wrote an essay for the Institute for the Study of Civil Society in 2000 in which she speaks most earnestly of her concerns for men today. She is uneasy to discover that so many fathers are denied their rights and that the swing of power to women has had appalling repercussions for the family. Pizzey says that even today people laugh when a man says he has been abused. But, she continues, 'I don't find any sort of abuse to any living thing a laughing matter'. She agrees, of course, that women who are on the receiving end of violence must be protected, but the programme she introduced was never intended to become one that some delinquent women could use against totally innocent men. When she tried to raise money to open a refuge for men in London, she could not get one single fundraiser to help her. Pizzey has firmly nailed her colours to the mast, making a stand against violence and in favour of justice for all.

The American Bar Association (ABA) has a website (www.abanet.org/domviol/home.html) with information about domestic violence, and a list of other very helpful links. One such link is the US National Domestic Violence Hotline. The ABA also posts a warning on its site about abusers discovering you have been looking for help on the Internet. They caution you to get rid of the 'history' on your computer, and suggest that to be absolutely safe it is best to go to a computer outside your home and do your Internet search from there. For immediate help in the US an important helpsite is Violence Against Women Online Resources at www.vaw.umn.edu.

Abuse Recovery UK (ARUK) at www.aruk.co.uk is a good place for survivors of abuse and their partners to gain support. This site is run by survivors for other survivors; they want anyone who has suffered abuse to know they are no longer alone. There is a list of helplines listed by county in the UK, and in the US by state. For those of you elsewhere Befrienders International (www.befrienders.org) is at your fingertips if you need speedy emotional help. Don't hesitate. There really is no need for you to feel that no one wants to listen to you. The World Health Organization has reported that in the last forty-five years the number of suicides has increased by 60 per cent, so if you or anyone you know is showing any signs of deep despair seek help immediately. It is a fallacy that people who talk about suicide don't do it. They can and they do. Another shocking statistic is that more people die each year from suicide than from homicide.

Telephone support is offered by the Jewish Marriage Council, which also has a crisis helpline. The service is called Miyad, which is Hebrew for 'immediate', and their principle is that there should be 'someone to talk to fast' (telephone: 020 8203 6211). The helpline is run by workers who go through rigorous training and selection. This is a national resource for all Jews regardless of religious commitment or practice.

Children can get depressed and anxious too. The telephone helpline Childline (0800 1111) receives far more calls each day than they can cope with, from anxious and troubled children of all ages. As a resource they are overstretched and it may be difficult to reach a counsellor. Childline acknowledges they cannot answer every call each day, so if you recognize a child who needs to talk, and often children do, urge them to keep trying to make contact. Other organizations such as YoungMinds, the mental health charity for children, will also advise about resources for kids. They have a Parents Information Service at the end of the telephone (0800 018 2138), and a website too (www.youngminds.org.uk). Contact them if you have any concerns about the mental health of a child or young person.

If you are wondering whether a child would benefit from psychotherapy, the Tavistock Clinic Adolescent/Child and Family Department has an international reputation for training and treatment. All referrals are under the NHS (which means they are free) and may be accepted from across the country, dependent upon an agreement with your local health authority. Referrals to the Adolescent Department may be made by adolescents themselves, parents, GPs or other professionals. The Department also provides a Young People's Counselling Service which is another self-referral service. Contact them by telephoning 020 7447 3714 for detailed information, if you are concerned about a young person in your care. Their website address is www.tmsi.org.uk.

Another point of contact is The British Association of Psychotherapists which has an assessment and treatment service for adolescents and children, as well as for adults. Their website address is www.bap-psychotherapy.org. They also offer some low fee psychotherapy treatment, and it is well worth getting information about their reduced fees scheme (telephone: 020 8452 9823). Treatment is given by senior students who will already have a previous qualification in psychology, medicine or social work, but who are still in training as psychotherapists. Through this scheme it is possible to get a very high standard of professional help at minimal cost, but there are only a few places available.

Do I need counselling?

If you have made the decision to look for a counsellor then take care over the next step. You may have a friend who can recommend someone, or your doctor may have a counsellor attached to the medical practice. If not, there are several highly reputable organizations which will help you. Don't be misled by advertisements in newspapers or magazines which promise a 'cure all'. There are safeguards for the public, and I recommend that you think about the qualification of your counsellor seriously. The best way to find a qualified counsellor in the UK is to ask for a referral from the British Association for Counselling and Psychotherapy. Any counsellor accredited to that organization has completed a recognized training and is governed by a strict code of ethics. Either telephone their headquarters (0870 4435252) or reach them on www.bac.co.uk.

A new resource in the US is www.counselors.com. How to find a counsellor is explained and there is also an entry to a 'public library' which consists of very helpful articles on a range of topics from grandparents raising grandkids and stepparenting to adolescent sexuality.

Counselling isn't something to be taken up lightly. The lengthy process entails looking at your own emotions which can be very painful. It can be hard to look at what propelled you to take a certain course of action at a particular time in your life. And it can be painful to realize what effect certain events in your life have had on you. But there are obvious advantages, as you may come to understand more about yourself than you anticipated or bargained for. Today more men and women are interested in self-knowledge than in a quick fix with medication. Prescribed drugs can sometimes offer symptomatic relief, but they do not solve problems of the heart any more than heroin or cocaine do. The similarity is that medically prescribed drugs, like any other kind of drug, are used to block out pain. If you have been prescribed sleeping pills or anti-depressants by your doctor you may need some help when you decide to stop taking them. So don't just give up 'taking the tablets' but consult your doctor about how to go about this.

Or a psychotherapist?

There is often some confusion about the difference between seeing a counsellor and seeing a psychotherapist. There is a fine line between one and the other. Training for the two professions often overlaps, which adds to the muddle. But a straightforward way of distinguishing between the two is to understand that a counsellor will be more directive, generally focussing on one aspect of your life and offering help with an immediate problem, such as bereavement. So, contacting an organization like Relate to see a marriage counsellor is often the first step if you want to talk over a relationship problem. The excellent team at Relate do not only help to 'mend' marriages, but can often assist couples to separate from each other in a healthy way too. Relate also runs a course to help people 'move on'. To find out more look in the yellow pages or on www.relate.org.uk.

A psychoanalytic-psychotherapist will help you untangle mixed feelings and emotions. A psychotherapist – which is what they are usually called, but which is unfortunately a label also used by many people who are not properly qualified – will assist you to understand how the feelings you now have became established and affect your behaviour without you realizing it. Psychotherapy is not concerned with quick problem solving but will patiently get to the root of the problem, so that you understand the unconscious pressures which motivate you. Psychotherapy is to be recommended if you want to work towards a fundamental change over a long period. The treatment will help you with a wide range of different changes which will last a lifetime. Therapy is not about helping someone make a particular decision. The aim is always greater. By developing self-awareness you will gain a wider perspective and be able to move towards making decisions. For example, if you have been through several failed or abusive relationships you may want to ask yourself '*Why* does my partner always treat me so badly?' And even to find the courage to ask 'Do I play any part in this, and if so *why*?' Psychotherapy over a long period will help you understand the answers to these questions. A vital ingredient in the process will be the relationship between you and your therapist. As the trust grows between you, so will your confidence in yourself, and this will bring about changes in your other relationships.

It can be hard to take the first step and to pick up the phone to make an appointment. You may well be answered by a machine, but don't be put off. If your therapist is working he or she will not interrupt a session with a patient or client to answer the phone. Either leave a message giving details of when you will be available, or try again later.

It can be quite daunting when you first meet with a counsellor or psychotherapist. You may be wondering what is expected of you. The answer is that at the consultation you do need to speak of the problems which have brought you to this point, to give the therapist some idea about you and the way you see things. Don't feel that you have to try to say everything which is on your mind. There will be plenty of time for that later. You may or may not want to tell the therapist something about your early upbringing and about major events in your life.

That first all-important meeting is for you both to get a *feel* for each other and to be comfortable about the idea of working together. Listen to what your therapist says to you and the way that it is said. Consider whether you like the approach and think about whether you feel heard. Trust your instincts about whether this professional is conscientious and reliable. All the professional training in the world cannot guarantee that this person has that special quality which makes a good therapist for *you*. Whether you decide to see a counsellor or a therapist the 'fit' between you must be right. But keep in mind you are not looking for a friend, but a professional person trained in the skills of counselling or therapy. It is essential that at this meeting some of the business side is discussed as well. How much will you be charged for a session, what happens if you miss a session, what happens if you take a holiday at a different time, will you have to pay if you are off sick, how will you be expected to pay? Don't be embarrassed to discuss these issues, your therapist won't be. Indeed, he or she will want you to be clear about them.

You may not at first be aware, for example, of the rule of paying for a missed session. There are sound reasons why patients are charged even if they don't come to a session: the therapist or counsellor will have reserved the time for you, and you alone. This will be 'your time', so although you may not feel this will ever apply to you, it would be all too easy if the going gets rough to skip appointments. Knowing that you will have to pay for the time anyway will help to make you think very seriously about cancelling or just not turning up for a session. It is all part of accepting the importance of the work, and appreciating the help of a highly trained professional. All these matters are best cleared up before the therapy or counselling begins. If you feel uneasy about any arrangements, you may want to consider seeing a different therapist before making a decision.

'I went to see a man I had heard of and found him cold and rather stern. The last thing I wanted at this time. I found the courage to tell him how I felt, and he suggested I see a colleague of his – a woman – and that felt right. I was very grateful about how things turned out.'

Together you will work out an agreed time or times for appointments. It is usual for a session to last for fifty minutes. Don't accept a time which you know from the start is going to be hard for you to keep. If you have a boss who will not let you be flexible with hours, then say so. Don't put yourself under additional strain by trying to slip out early every Friday afternoon, or coming in late every Tuesday morning! Either wait until you can be offered a more convenient time, or speak to your boss and make an arrangement.

Even if during the consultation you feel the fit between you and the therapist is right and the times offered are manageable and convenient, ask if you can have a day to think it over. Your therapist or counsellor will appreciate the fact that you are taking this commitment seriously, and not jumping in feet first without considering the consequences.

'I had a consultation to find out what I wanted – counselling or therapy. The assessor suggested psychotherapy because we agreed I wanted help to sort out quite a few problems which worried me. The first day I saw a therapist I just knew it was right, and three years on I can see how so much has changed in me. I wish I had gone years ago.'

'I saw a counsellor for four months. I couldn't see the point of discussing my early family life. I just needed to get my feet back on the ground and move on. He helped me a lot.'

> *'I decided on therapy. Oh the feeling of relief when I lay on the couch and could say all the things that were on my mind in my own time. Friends and family kept telling me what to do and giving advice. My therapist just listened to me in a way that made me feel listened to properly for the first time in my life.'*

In therapy there is more emphasis on understanding the unconscious processes, and treatment can take a long time. This must be taken into consideration when you are thinking of which path to take – counselling or psychotherapy?

> *'I laughed out loud at the thought of seeing a therapist three times a week. What would I talk about? Anyway, I thought I'd have a go and haven't looked back since.'*
>
> *'What I appreciated was that I could be silent if I wished. Before I started I wouldn't have understood that this is healing too. Knowing that there is someone there, but that that someone won't keep asking questions or just talking and will give you all the time you need, is wonderful.'*
>
> *'I saw a counsellor at my university after Bob left. After a dozen sessions I did feel better, and later that year decided to look for some psychotherapy.'*

This last comment is not unusual. Frequently someone who feels they have been helped by counselling, perhaps sorting out an immediate problem, later wants to go into things more deeply and opts for psychotherapy.

How much will it cost?

In the UK the free counselling or psychotherapy services are very patchy and searching for them takes tenacity and is often a frustrating experience. You may find your GP's practice has a counsellor or a psychologist attached, but if so you may only be offered a limited number of sessions. It may be possible for your doctor to refer you to a nearby hospital which has a Psychotherapy Department. Or your company may have a staff counsellor. There are several very good organizations, and I list some which seem to me to offer a high standard of care. Some of these organizations offer specialist help in the way of religious or cultural understanding.

- **The Westminster Pastoral Foundation** (020 7937 6956) has its headquarters in Kensington and there are affiliated centres in different parts of the country. This national organization which trains counsellors and psychotherapists also has a clinical service. Their counsellors are trained in the psychodynamic approach to counselling and psychotherapy. Everyone requesting help is asked to come for an initial assessment session and the cost of this ranges from £45 for those in full-time employment to £15 for those unemployed or unwaged. Clients may be seen either by a staff counsellor or a trainee counsellor. The WPF does have some low fee paying clients, and they have four fee bands ranging from full cost to low cost. The actual cost of each individual counselling session is in the region of £40 for a fifty-minute session, and £25 for a group session of 1½ hours.

- **The Jewish Marriage Council** is a great source of different counselling help: mediation, solo workshops, individual counselling and other services are available. The JMC have a sliding scale of payment for counselling, down to zero for special cases. Their slogan is one I find very welcoming: 'When you don't know who to trust, you can turn to us'. They are available whatever stage your relationship has reached, and can offer appointments in London and in Manchester. The national appointments line is 0845 585 159. The solo workshops are to enable you to 'come to terms with the past, look forward to the future'. These workshops run for seven two-hour sessions, and while the cost has been set at an affordable level, reductions are available for those in special circumstance so that no one who wants to attend is excluded. If you are Jewish, on your own, and determined to come to terms with a relationship breakdown and look to the future, I would suggest you find out more about these workshops.

There is also an outreach programme of the Jewish Marriage Council called CLASP (Community Link Awareness for Single Parents), specifically to address the many unacknowledged problems which face single parents within the Jewish community. They acknowledge that there are more single parent families today and the number continues to grow. For more information contact Lilian Brodie at 020 8203 6311.

- **The Association of Christian Counsellors** is there if you want to look for Christian Counselling. Contact www.doveuk.com or telephone 0118 966 2207. They are not officially a referral agency, but they have set up a system manned by volunteers who will put people in touch with suitable counsellors. Details are also available from them about Christian Counsellors in Europe and beyond.

  Dedicated to marriage, www.2-in-2-1.co.uk is a site strongly supporting marriage. It also has details about Christian Counselling, a Marriage Clinic, and tips on Marital First Aid.

  Connections Christian Counselling is a website organized by two members of the Baptist Church (www.connections.ndirect .co.uk). For a fee they offer some pre-marriage help. For more information e-mail info@connections-c.co.uk.

- **The Muslim Women's Helpline** has been in operation since 1987 and is there to help with problems of sexual abuse, domestic violence and marital problems, including forced marriage. According to their leaflet they aim to be involved with 'changing our community for the better, one woman's life at a time'. The MWHL provides a telephone service and, where appropriate, face-to-face counselling for all Muslim women, whatever their cultural, ethnic or linguistic background. Their service is available from 10.00–16.00, Monday to Friday at 020 8904 8193. It is operated by volunteers with a wide range of qualifications and expertise; all are trained to give non-judgmental Islamic counselling. They report a worrying increase in the number of calls per year about domestic violence, sexual abuse and problems related to converts and forced marriage. They feel that the women who contact them appreciate talking to someone with the same religious values. When I telephoned their helpline for information about their service I spoke with the woman who answered my call at length, and I felt I was met with great warmth and courtesy. So if this is where you need to turn, don't hesitate.

- **The Asian Family Counselling Service** is a confidential counselling service for families, couples and individuals of the Asian community. Help is provided in the Asian languages by trained counsellors. They will also see couples where one partner is Asian. They see many clients with family and marital difficulties and deal with issues to do with arranged and forced marriages. There are no charges for weekday sessions, but there is a charge (on a sliding scale) for evening and weekend sessions. Telephone 020 8567 5616 between 9 and 12 noon for an appointment or write to 76 Church Road, Hanwell, London W7 1LB.

- **With Dignity** is another organization which is a non-profit, registered charity aiming to help and support people who are coming to terms with the ending of a relationship through adultery, general breakdown or divorce. They have a freephone helpline (0800 085 0424) and nationwide groups. In order to join a group you need to become a member of WITH DIGNITY, and the cost of this is £25 per annum. For that you will also get a newsletter giving details of social events and contact numbers of other members who are there to offer support. As with most organizations they have an e-mail address for general information (info@withdignity.org.uk).

- **The British Association of Psychotherapists**, as mentioned earlier, is a leading organization training both adult and child psychotherapists; it also has a clinical service. Through them it is possible to arrange for an assessment. Such a consultation, with a skilled practitioner and before a referral is made, has been shown to be useful. The cost of an assessment is £40 and for ongoing treatment the cost is between £35 and £40 per session. In addition, the BAP has a reduced fee scheme for both adults and children where the cost is £6 to £15 per session depending upon financial circumstances. Information about these services can be obtained direct from the BAP (telephone: 020 8452 9823).

Group therapy

If individual counselling or therapy does not appeal to you, you may consider group therapy. A therapy group can provide a safe setting where thoughts, feelings and experiences can be shared. The interaction between the group members is part of the treatment and gradually more self-awareness is developed through this experience. A group can be an excellent place to learn about feelings and relationships. As with individual help you will have to search around to see what is available in your area. Sometimes local groups will have a notice in the public library or on the noticeboard in your doctor's surgery.

- **The Group-Analytic Practice** is a good starting point. This organization is in a central position in London. The core of their work is ongoing group psychotherapy in once-weekly, twice-weekly and weekend block groups, as well as groups for couples. The GAP has single-sex groups as well as mixed groups. They offer a thorough psychotherapeutic assessment to ensure the best fit between a patient's needs and the type of therapy group. Their fee for an individual consultation is £100 and for couples £90 to £130. The cost for a once-weekly group is £97 per month and for couples £200 per month. Telephone 020 7935 3103 or visit their website (www.gapractice.org.uk).

- **The Institute of Group Analysis** (www.igalondon.org.uk) has a list of members who conduct private groups throughout the UK. On their website they say they will offer advice and information over the phone about psychotherapy and give help in finding a therapist if you want to join a group. Telephone 020 7431 2693 for information.

- **The Phoenix Divorce Recovery** is worth considering if you live in London. This is a fifteen-week programme of recovery. They say you will receive 'help, guidance and support and develop new strategies to overcome fears and rejection, deal with anger and loss and re-establish your self esteem'. For information and details of the next course telephone 020 8893 9665.

- **The Divorce Recovery Workshop** is a UK nationwide self-help group run by volunteers. There is no 'expert' to lead the groups (which consist of six weekly sessions) but they are all run by people who have experienced the break-up of their own relationship. They have been in existence since 1992 and have flourished across the country. I like their motto too: 'Don't just go through it – grow through it'. They organize occasional long-weekend, residential workshops and more information about locations of the groups can be found on their website at www.drw.org.uk or by contacting their national telephone number (07000 781 889).

If you hope to get help for at least some of the cost of therapy from your private health insurer, make sure you check with them first. Different organizations have different rules, so beware of the small print. Some insurers offer help for a limited time, others seem to be more generous. But find out their regulations before embarking on your search for a counsellor or therapist.

Do you need counselling or therapy:

- Do you have feelings of deep despair out of proportion to your situation?
- Do your feelings of loss and mourning get heavier as time goes by?
- Do you feel your divorce has made you wary of getting involved with someone new?
- Do you feel you are a burden to your friends and family?
- Do you find you are plagued with extreme tiredness, but can't sleep through the night?
- Do you feel 'under the weather' most of the time?
- Do you still feel the need to talk excessively about your life?
- Do you want to know more about yourself, and the way you 'tick'?
- Do you want to know more about the way events and relationships in your life have affected you?
- Do you think you could feel relief from talking to someone who is not personally involved in any way with the break-up?
- Do you long to be able to talk to someone who will listen to you, and not in turn burden you with their problems?

If the answer is 'yes' to more than half of these questions, consider quite seriously the question of finding some psychological help.

There are innumerable organizations in the US and I suggest a good starting point is THE NATIONAL GROUP PSYCHOTHERAPY INSTITUTE. Their website (www.wspsych.com) gives detailed information about groups and training.

Where can you find help:

- **The Internet** There are many excellent sites offering support and a chance to chat to others who have had similar experiences.
- **Helplines** These are manned by volunteers on the whole, and you will always find a sympathetic ear on the end of a telephone to listen to you. So never feel totally on your own with a problem or that there is no one in the world interested in hearing what you have to say.
- **Counselling** If you want to talk to someone who will listen and help you to work through difficulties which are weighing you down, look for a counsellor. But – most important – make sure you are seeing a counsellor trained by a reputable organization.
- **Psychotherapy** If you truly want to understand more about the way you feel and think, and to understand more about unconscious processes, then therapy is for you. The qualifications and training of the person you see are most important and the safest way to find a therapist is through a training organization followed by a consultation. Make sure you feel comfortable with your therapist, and don't agree to any arrangements which make you feel uneasy in any way.
- **Group Therapy** You may prefer to consider taking part in a group where interaction with other group members will also help you to develop self-awareness and insight and to foster personal growth and change. Groups may often have a common core – such as a women's group, or divorce recovery.

9

Do you need legal advice?

A lawyer with his briefcase can steal more
than a hundred men with guns.
(Mario Puzo, *The Godfather*)

Looking on the Internet

There are many sites on the Internet which offer legal advice and guidance on the practical details of getting a divorce. If you do not have ready access to the Internet it is well worth your time to collate some of the following addresses and information and to visit an Internet cafe so that you can log on. In this way much information is available at the touch of a button.

Make sure that the advice you are looking at relates to the country, and in the US even the state, you live in. Also, that the information is up-to-date. The website Divorce Online (www.divorce-online.co.uk) offers comprehensive advice about self-help for men and women living in England and Wales. For those in the US, a good site to visit is Divorce Doc (www.divorcedoc.com) where there is plenty to read, and where there are pointers to further advice and resources in each state.

A good source of legal information about many different issues is www.freelawyer.co.uk. This site has a questionnaire you can complete and based on the information you give them they will provide a print-out of information relevant to your situation, couched in language a layman can understand. This is truly an interactive website – but they do warn that their service is no substitute for seeing a lawyer face to face. Meanwhile, you will learn a great deal. Another site giving free legal advice for England and Wales is Community Legal Services (www.justask.org.uk). As their web address indicates, you just have to ask whatever it is you need to know more about.

The advice the websites spell out is clear and to the point. Reading the facts will alert you to some of the do's and don't's about getting a divorce and will give you more of an idea about the issues you will be facing. However, it is as well to keep in mind that the online information is usually a general guide only, and that you should think seriously about taking professional advice relating to your own circumstances. If you make thorough notes about what you need to have clarified it will make your appointment with any legal advisor quicker, more to the point, and certainly cheaper.

Take care that if you go to see a legal professional you don't make the mistake of thinking that you are talking to a counsellor. Stick to the facts – the clock will be ticking and most solicitors have an hourly rate. Don't be afraid to talk about costs when you make contact, and ask your solicitor to explain to you whether you are entitled to some aid. What used to be called 'legal aid' in the UK is now called 'public funding'. Depending on your income you may be eligible for some help towards the cost of the divorce. Ask to have this explained in full, because some of the funding may be treated as a loan – to be paid back later from your assets. If you have received financial aid and you are then awarded more than £2,500 in your settlement, you will be liable for charges. So beware! Asking about costs must be near the top of your list.

Look, too, for information about voluntary organizations which offer help. Public libraries are often an excellent source for information about where to go for advice locally. For example, in the UK find out the address of your nearest Citizen's Advice Bureau. Or visit their site on www.nacab.org.uk for more information about help on offer. Don't neglect the Law Centres which give quality service if you cannot afford to consult a solicitor, or if you need to seek specialist advice about a specific problem. These are two sound sources of help which are often overlooked in the heat of the moment.

On the whole, divorces – though initially instigated by one partner – are eventually settled by agreement. Contested divorces are very rare, and very costly. You have probably heard horror stories of divorces which dragged on 'for years', but this is unlikely to happen if you and your ex can forge some kind of agreement and settlement. It is difficult to put the words 'amicable' and 'divorce' together in the same sentence, but whatever your particular situation, it is in your best interest to keep things as calm and peaceful as possible. Do keep in mind that direct dialogue with your ex is *always* best. Select a moment to talk when you are feeling at your strongest, work out in advance what you need to discuss together, and keep to that agenda.

If you are a parent and looking for a solicitor there are many good reasons why you should choose a member of the Solicitors' Family Law Association (www.sfla.co.uk or telephone 01689 850227) who have over 4000 members in the UK. These solicitors are trained to deal with family disputes and will help you to seek a fair solution. Their aim is a just settlement rather than expensive and unnecessary litigation. It is important that you have a solicitor who will make sure you understand the consequences of any decisions and the effect on any children involved. This way you and your ex are more likely to arrive at a satisfactory solution at less cost, both emotionally and financially. Bear in mind that agreed solutions are more likely to be kept to over the years than those imposed by a court. This is especially important when making decisions about the children.

It is possible to issue a divorce yourself, and again there is information available on the Internet about how to go about this. But it is advisable to get legal advice to avoid complications, especially if there are children and/or property or financial concerns which complicate the matter.

It is only in exceptional circumstances that you will be required to appear in court, and it is most likely that all the paperwork can be done by post. You can get a form from your county court. If you have children you will also need a form to complete called 'Statement of Arrangements'. Hopefully this is something you and your partner can complete together. If you are making the application to the court, you will be the Petitioner. This Petition together with a reply form and the Statement of Arrangements is sent to your spouse. If there is agreement, then things can proceed fairly swiftly. There may be objections from your spouse about costs, and if there is any animosity or malice there can be delaying tactics which are often hard to bear. The next stage is for you to apply for a decree nisi which is a declaration that your marriage has irretrievably broken down. Once this has been granted by the court you are free after six weeks to apply for a decree absolute. With the receipt of this document you are no longer married.

No doubt you will already have considered changing any will you made while married. If you do not do this and you die before the divorce is final, then at least part of your estate will pass to your spouse.

On the Internet you can search for help about a religious divorce. For instance, the Jewish Marriage Guidance Council (JMGC) are there on-line (and on the end of the telephone) to spell out how to go about obtaining a 'Get'. Without this bill of divorcement no Jew may remarry within the Jewish faith. The very real difficulty arises from the Jewish belief that there should be no marriage without consent and likewise no divorce without consent. As the Get must be applied for by the man and given to the woman, there are women who find themselves in a dreadful position. They may have obtained their civil divorce, but if an ex-husband refuses to give his ex-wife a religious divorce, it has fundamentally restrictive consequences for her future, since a remarriage in an orthodox synagogue is forbidden and a civil marriage will not be recognized in Jewish law. This means that all children of the woman's subsequent marriage will be seen as illegitimate according to the Jewish faith and so will their children. The JMGC is there to offer advice and support and they will negotiate with an unhelpful husband. Their aim is to help remove any obstruction to the cooperation needed to attain a religious divorce. Many Jewish women today find this situation unacceptable and have banded together for mutual support. They are called Agunahs, chained women, and hope to persuade the rabbis to change their interpretation of the laws about marriage. For support in the UK visit www.agunot.co.uk and for more information worldwide see www.agunot-campaign.org.uk.

If you need advice about marriage or remarriage from a Catholic standpoint, a very helpful site on the Internet is Catholic Digest (www.catholicdigest.org). There is an excellent marriage quiz (www.catholicdigest.org/stories199706066a.html) where you can read questions (and answers) to such vexing questions as 'If a Catholic marries a non-Catholic outside the Church and then the couple divorces, is the Catholic free to marry in Church without an annulment?' The answer, you may be surprised to learn, is 'No'. You may need to know about the way to seek an annulment. This begins at parish level, and then proceeds to the Diocesan Court. An annulment means having the Church examine the relationship closely and fully. Fees charged for this are to cover the costs only.

Another legal term you may have heard some people speak about is a 'judicial separation' and you may not be clear what this is. It means that two people have decided to live apart and they wish to make the separation more formal, while not actually filing for divorce. This means that the couple remain married, but all marital obligations come to an end. They are no longer obliged to live together, and neither spouse will benefit automatically from the other's will in the event of a death. Unless, of course, a new will has been drawn up stating this desire. A judicial separation gives the court the same powers to divide matrimonial property as it has in the case of a divorce. The main reason to opt for a judicial separation is when one of the couple is opposed to divorce, and the reason for this is usually a religious one. Another reason can be if there is a break in a marital relationship in the first year of marriage when a divorce is not an option in the UK. There are not many judicial separations each year in comparison with the number of divorces granted. If your partner is asking you to agree to this way of untangling your marriage, you would be well advised to seek legal opinion before consenting. Do not agree to anything in haste, or in the mistaken belief it will make things easier in the long run.

Mediation

In 1996 the Family Law Act was introduced with the intention of making divorce less acrimonious by allowing couples to end their marriage after one year (or eighteen months for those couples with children) without the need to cite adultery or other fault. At the time this was welcomed as the 'no fault' divorce which would make divorce less traumatic for all concerned. By introducing 'information meetings' for all couples wanting a divorce it was believed that some marriages could be saved and couples who were uncertain about what they wanted would be helped to seek counselling. 'Mediation' was the buzz word, rather than 'lawyers'. However, this did not go to plan and research shows that after a meeting the importance of retaining a lawyer was reinforced. It is sad that a way of making divorce less bitter did not materialize. Although the idea of 'no fault' divorce was initially backed by lawyers the Act itself was described as a dog's breakfast. It seems that the original thinking behind it was gradually diluted in order to please different groups of people who all had different ideas about marriage, and certainly about divorce. The scheme has now been abandoned as unworkable and too costly.

It is often argued that anything that reduces the pain of divorce also undermines the institution of marriage and, indeed, the fabric of our society. The whole question of how much politicians should become involved in 'the family' has become an area of disagreement for professionals from many different disciplines. However, no one can believe that a long drawn out battle over children or property can help anybody at all in the end.

There has often been confusion between mediation and counselling. Mediation is not intended to help to mend a marriage. The purpose of mediation is to help couples end their marriage in a less embittered way. However, not many couples opt for mediation when they have decided to divorce. It is often too late at that point.

> 'I didn't want the divorce from the start, but once we were so far down the road I knew there was no turning back, I certainly didn't want to talk to anyone else about it.'
>
> 'I hated the idea of him leaving me. I ended up hating him. No way did I want to talk any more.'

The organization National Family Mediation (www.nfm.u-net.com or telephone 020 7383 5993) has a very helpful leaflet called *Divorcing or Separating?* It explains what family mediation is and what it isn't. You might find it interesting and reassuring to see in black and white that mediation is not about reconciliation or about legal matters. It is not about taking sides. Mediation is about helping families affected by divorce or separation and the major changes they bring. It can be very helpful for couples who are at war as parents to meet with a mediator (for up to six sessions) to discuss arrangements for the children. The NFM believes that they can help parents who are apart to stay close to their children. It makes no difference whether you have been married or cohabiting or whether or not you have children. However, the essential ingredient must be that both want to go to a meeting and see the sense of it.

The African Caribbean Family Mediation Service is there to help separated parents make arrangements for their children, and it aims to reduce conflict and to help parents to recognize the needs of their children rather than the problems that exist between them. You will be seen by fully trained African/Caribbean family mediators providing a service which is ethically and culturally sensitive to your needs. Remember, mediators are always impartial, and they do not take sides or judge between you. Family mediators are there to help you reach decisions and formulate your own agreements. They will not take decisions for you. Their fees are modest at £5 to £27 per person per session. Telephone 020 7737 2366 for more information or write to The African Caribbean Family Mediation Service, 2–4 St John's Crescent, Brixton, SW9 7LZ. This organization also operates a child contact centre. Any parent who has a contact or access agreement with the other parent can use the centre. Grandparents, uncles and aunts can also use the centre to meet grandchildren, nieces and nephews as long as agreement has been reached with the parent caring for the child. The contact centre can also undertake to supervise meetings between parents and children.

> 'I was all for it. I knew he wouldn't shout at me if there was someone else there. He had to listen to me. Great.'
>
> 'I went along reluctantly and didn't see what it was all about, really.'

It may seem a little late in the day to mention this, but The Catholic Engagement Encounter (www.engagedencounter.org) offers a place for couples to discuss their idea of what marriage means. I very much like their motto: 'A wedding is a day: a marriage is a lifetime'.

Cohabitation

Over the years there has been an increase in the numbers of couples who cohabit. Or as some people prefer to call it, live as an 'unmarried couple household'.

If you have not been married, you may still find it is difficult to untangle your lives in a legal way, not only in an emotional way. It is a surprise for some couples who have been living together for many years to discover that there are specific hurdles to overcome. If you have lived together for years you may think that you will be treated as if you have been married. This is not so.

What if you have property owned jointly? Perhaps when buying things you gave careful thought to what would happen if one of you died, or in the event you decided to separate. If you did not think of these possibilities, then it is important now to obtain a legal opinion. In fact anyone thinking of cohabiting would be wise from the beginning to have some kind of formal written agreement about what is to happen should they later decide to part. However, these couples may be the very ones who do not want to formalize their relationships in any way and that is why they are not taking part in a marriage ceremony. Just because you have not married, it doesn't mean you will not have to go through the different hoops of a 'divorce' or break-up. If you do not have an agreement there is often little support if a relationship breaks down. You could end up losing the lot.

> *'When we decided to live together I wouldn't have dreamt of asking Bill to sign a written agreement. Fifteen years later we both wish we had had that foresight.'*

Maintenance cannot be claimed from an ex-partner if you have not married, and you break up. Recently though, there have been several high profile cases where 'palimony' has been awarded after the break-up of a common-law relationship. Keep in mind that if one person in an unmarried relationship dies the other does not have an automatic right to their estate. Again, it is important to seek legal advice about these issues.

> *'We lived together for seventeen years before he left me. I was staggered to find that I was not considered to be his wife. Something like this had never occurred to me.'*

In a small number of states in America the status of a common-law relationship is recognized as an 'informal' marriage and therefore certain legal rights and protections are acknowledged. However, most states do not recognize common-law marriages. It is very important that you get a legal opinion about your rights. You will find, though, that the lack of a wedding does not make ending a relationship easier or trouble free.

If you are considering cohabiting in the future www.divorce-online.co.uk gives you information in a Cohabitation Agreement Legalpac. It will help a court to reach a fair decision should troubles arise.

What happens if you have children?

The basis of parental rights in the UK today is that married couples have 'parental responsibility', which means that both parents have responsibility for making decisions about how the children are brought up. If you have not been married the situation is different. Quite often no problems arise until a couple who have been cohabiting decide to separate. The bald fact is that an unmarried father has no legal rights in England and Wales, although he is not exempt from paying child support.

If you are an unmarried father it may come as a shock to know that only the mother has automatic parental responsibility. The mother can, however, agree that this should be widened to include the father. If a mother refuses, the unmarried father may fight for this status and can apply to a court for a Parental Responsibility Agreement, which grants the unmarried father almost the same rights in bringing up a child as a married father. Neither does a stepfather automatically have parental responsibility, but again he can appeal to the court for this order. If this is your situation, you will find support and advice from Families Need Fathers (FNF). According to FNF 40 per cent of separated fathers lose all contact with their children two years after a divorce. Don't become one of those statistics. The European Parliament has approved a series of new measures aimed at strengthening European Community law on access. The regulation will apply to all children under the age of sixteen whose parents have had a divorce or legal separation within the community.

Whether it is you or your partner who wants the divorce, the arrangements about the children should if possible be agreed in advance. The court will need to be satisfied that there have been agreements about where the children will live, and about their contact with the other parent. If you cannot both agree upon a plan, then you will be asked to discuss the situation with a mediator. Court proceedings are usually only issued when there are difficulties about a specific issue, such as taking the children abroad. If disagreement still remains then a Family Court Welfare Officer will become involved in an effort to find some common ground. At all times the court will judge the welfare of the children to be top priority, and depending upon the children's ages, their thoughts and feelings will be taken into account.

If you or your children have been subjected to any violence, then you may decide that the children should only have contact with the other parent at a supervised location. This is where the contact centres can be helpful in easing this situation. The National Association of Child Contact Centres (NACCC) prides itself on 'bridging the break-up' and they currently help to keep 2,000 children a week in touch with both parents. Violence is not, of course, the only reason why parents may decide on this way forward. Consult the NACCC for more information and locations. You can telephone them on 0115 948 4557 or go to their website at www.naccc.org.uk.

Accusations of fear of violence or abuse may be used as a weapon to prevent a parent from seeing his kids. If you are a parent who is having difficulty in seeing your children it is wise to agree, even as a temporary measure, to see your children at a contact centre. They are friendly places, which enable you to keep the communication going with your children.

> '*Thank God I saw them at a centre. It all got sorted out eventually but in the meantime it meant I could see them each weekend. I wouldn't be surprised to hear many fathers give up hope and just opt out. The accusations against me were terrible.*'

Child Support Agency

In the UK the job of this government department is to assess, collect and pay child support maintenance. Since its creation in 1993 it has faced many difficulties and has often received a very bad press. The agency's brief is to ensure that parents who live apart from their family meet their financial responsibilities to their children. At first this was universally welcomed, but so many flaws appeared that everyone's confidence in this department was shaken. The CSA works out payment from a formula, i.e, they have a standard figure of how much the allowance should be for a child, and they take into account a number of other factors. The system is very complicated indeed and has often been seen to work unfairly. Because of this there are government plans to simplify the formula in 2002. The CSA have enormous powers to take money from wages, seize money or goods, even your house. Ignore the CSA at your peril. The Act which was brought about in a wave of publicity to find 'dead-beat dads' and to make them pay has misfired terribly on many families. Dads who have willingly completed the maintenance enquiry form find later they have given the CSA more information than they need have done, and it can't be undone.

The latest ruling is that men who refuse the Child Support Agency's demands for a DNA test will be automatically ruled to be a child's father. The CSA have been given wide-ranging powers to make sure there is no hiding place, at home or overseas, for fathers who abscond. Soldiers serving abroad will be particularly targeted in an effort to force fathers to face up to their responsibilities. The department has a new power to confiscate the driving licences of fathers who refuse to pay maintenance. It will also become a criminal offence to withhold information without reasonable excuse or to supply false information to the CSA.

In addition, the agency will presume parentage where a man is married to the mother at any time between conception and birth of the child, or registered as the father on the birth certificate. The voices speaking up against these stern measures are from organizations which believe they will further alienate some fathers. The publicity which surrounds these new measures also reinforces for many people that 'all' fathers are trying to avoid their financial obligations and this is far from the case. It is grossly unfair to portray all fathers as men who are dodging family responsibilities. A very real difficulty arises if you have a new partner, with or without children, who has earnings of her own. This is where the unfairness often bites hardest. If you have shared care of the children this too will affect the CSA assessment. If you are about to be involved with the Agency it is wise to get professional advice (the Citizens Advice Bureau will be able to help you). Many dads who feel they have been unjustly assessed appeal to their Member of Parliament. Visit the CSA on-line for information, and to read their Charter which can be found on www.dhssni.gov.uk/child_support/publications/charter/index.html. Have a look, too, at the independent website (www.willow981.freeserve.co.uk) which is a guide for victims of the UK Child Support Agency. It will give you an overall view of the pitfalls to look out for.

As a mother, tell the CSA if you are in fear of violence from your child's father. Ask for a 'good cause' interview. You will find them sympathetic to this situation.

It is not obligatory to use the CSA if you can agree between yourselves about the amount of maintenance to be paid voluntarily. Any arrangements you and your partner can agree upon together make for happier relationships in the long run.

Pension Rights

From December 2000 there has been the *option* to divide pensions at the time of the divorce. This applies only to England and Wales. However, the whole question of the value of pensions, and different types of pensions, means you would be well advised to consult an independent financial advisor.

There are several alternatives available to you whether you are considering your own pension rights or are the potential recipient of pension rights after a divorce. Pension rights, and the matrimonial home, are usually the two biggest assets to be split after a divorce and care should be taken about any decisions. A helpful source of information is the government's impartial pension information site (www.pensionguide.co.uk). Gather as many facts as you can.

If you are uncertain about your position with the Inland Revenue and need more help about self-assessment, national insurance contributions or tax credits, go to www.inlandrevenue.gov.uk/home.htm. They also have leaflets on hand to show you how benefits are affected if your marriage ends in divorce or annulment.

The Financial Services Authority (www.fsa.gov.uk/consumer) offers a wide range of options to help you to plan your financial future and you would be well advised to consider different choices. Get copies of the booklets and fact sheets they offer.

Tips on seeking legal advice:

- Search the Internet for sites offering legal advice, but only as a first step.
- Then consider making an appointment to see a professional to discuss specific issues.
- At the start of any consultation with a professional discuss the likely cost.
- Find out if you are you eligible for financial help.
- Don't be afraid to ask questions, and be sure you understand what you are agreeing to.

- Remake your will.
- Do your utmost to come to an agreement about the children before the divorce.
- Remember that mediation and counselling are two different things. Don't confuse them.
- Keep in mind that the hurdles to overcome are not the same for those who have been cohabiting rather than married.
- If there are difficulties about arranging to see your children ask if you can meet them at a contact centre.
- Make sure all joint accounts are closed. Do you have shared store accounts?
- Keep a detailed list of all expenses. Include everyday necessities such as food, insurance, fares, pet food, cleaning materials, personal items, school trips, birthday presents, cinema tickets, newspapers, plants and flowers, children's pocket money, prescription charges, shoe repairs, hairdressers, stamps, dentist – the list will seem endless once you start.
- Consult an independent financial advisor, especially about pension rights and options.

Part Four

It's All Behind You Now

For a while we pondered whether to take a vacation or get a divorce. We decided that a trip to Bermuda is over in two weeks but a divorce is something you always have.

(Woody Allen)

10

Ready for the future

Be thou the rainbow in the storms of life. The evening beam that smiles the clouds away, and tints tomorrow with prophetic ray.

(Byron)

Another chance?

We have now travelled together down a long and winding road. Let's just have a look at how far we have come. You may have reversed the direction you planned to take, and your energies may have been successfully ploughed back into your relationship. You may have found that although this relationship was in crisis it did not have to slide out of control. Learning that couples who are happily married stay healthier and live longer may have influenced your decision to have another go. Couples who remain married to each other are better off financially too! Perhaps you looked at the checklist on page 56 and more yes's than no's encouraged you to have another shot. Unfortunately, many of you will not be able to take this course.

This book would not have caught your eye if you had not been feeling something was wrong. All couples need to take care of their marriages, but it is surprising how many men and women just get on with day-to-day life and hope for the best. The saddest situation is to believe that because your marriage has somehow reached the doldrums there is nothing to be done and you have to put up with it. Too many people have thought this and then been totally surprised and shocked when it is their partner who decides to leave. If the blow comes through the discovery of an extramarital affair this can set you reeling. This will be heightened by being told that the reason your partner became involved with someone else was because it made him feel 'alive again', someone was 'interested' in him at a time he felt most lonely, or he realized that there had to be a major 'change' in his life.

Only later can it be accepted by both partners that there must have been something missing in the marriage for there to be room for that 'someone else'. Maybe a gap has opened between you so that you both lose touch, and stop listening to the dreams of the other. Another heartbreaking cause for relationships to break apart is a crisis in the family, perhaps the death of a child.

If you feel that your marriage has reached a low ebb, then don't be complacent. Do something about it *now*. Don't wait until a divorce is inevitable. The knack is to realize that during the course of a marriage things change. No one should expect to live at the thrilling height which you experienced when you first fell in love. Sex does not stay at the same intensity for most couples, despite what your friends might tell you. A thousand and one things crowd into your mind each day, especially if you have a demanding job and/or children to bring up. But do you recall how when you first met your partner you were thinking of each other most of the day, and sometimes part of the night? Remember how you spent hours planning a surprise deciding what to buy your lover for a birthday present? Although it would be unrealistic to think that life could go on at this pace, ask yourself when you last made that spontaneous gesture towards your partner which is a way of signalling love and affection. Have you allowed your life together to become predictable and stale? A good loving relationship brings out the best in us; it is also what contributed to your feeling of well-being when you fell in love. Slowly falling out of love brings with it the opposite feelings. Often these are experienced as aches and pains, or even depression. The desire to recapture that loving feeling accounts for many extramarital relationships.

When we fall in love we feel more complete, and this in turn fosters the belief that we really do need that other person in order to survive. So why do so many of us become careless and let that devotion slip away? When the death of a spouse was the most frequent cause of the end of a relationship there may have been no time to brood over the quality of a marriage. In earlier times death solved the problems for some couples. Today we live longer, we are healthier and we have been led to believe that we have a 'right' to happiness. So is it too much to ask of a young couple to make a lifetime commitment to each other? In the best of all possible worlds this would not be so. However, the world we live in is far from that, and life today is not so straightforward.

I don't believe that many couples enter into marriage expecting that they will get divorced. But no one can anticipate what the future may throw at them. Lengthy marriages are about weathering good and bad times, and getting the balance right. Some couples can stay strong together and happily celebrate their silver, golden, and even diamond wedding anniversaries. I don't believe for a moment they have had an especially easy ride, but somehow they have managed to hold on to each other and to survive, even thrive, on the merry-go-round of married life. If we could know their secret, and bottle it, we could make a fortune. But we can't, and so each couple has to find its own way. There is an old wives' saying that no one really knows what goes on behind a closed bedroom door, except the couple themselves. This is true; we do not know, even though you may hear a one-sided version from a friend! There is an equally astute old saying that if everything is alright in the bedroom it is alright in the other rooms of the house. This applies not just to sex and making love, but to sharing intimacy of every kind. I can lay down suggestions and flag possible danger areas to watch out for, but at the end of the day there has to be understanding between partners, sensitivity to each other's feelings, and a *belief* in each other. An ability to laugh together doesn't hurt either.

We all need to feel we are cared about. In this busy world, if we want to form a relationship which lasts, we have to carve out time to show our partner we care, that we care very much indeed. We need to change step when events bring about a different chapter in our lives. If a couple can keep in unison as they move from the early days of being a couple – perhaps then becoming parents and eventually being a couple in retirement – and keep their love for each other fresh and alive, they are lucky indeed.

I wonder why, when we are faced by the dreadful statistics for divorce, most of us still have trust in marriage. Is it because we believe in love? The Western idea of a love match still holds firm, but even with the field wide open many make mistakes, some more than once. I believe this is because our choice of partner is coloured by many conscious and unconscious factors. For example, did you want your marriage to be a carbon copy of your parents' relationship, or quite the opposite, or have you tried to create a union best suited to you and your partner?

I have repeatedly emphasised the importance of talking to your partner. Let me reinforce once again that when I say *talk*, I don't just mean sharing information. If you don't tell your partner how you are feeling, or listen to what your partner may be trying to tell you, something will have to give. And it might be the marriage.

There are many barriers to communication; one obstacle might be an inability to take into account the other's point of view. Can you put yourself in your partner's shoes and see what your relationship must look like from his angle? Of course, it is a mistake only to wear his shoes and to lose sight of what *you* want out of life. If you do that, you may have become like many women and live 'through' your partner, and possibly your children too. In an earlier chapter we heard from one woman who said that after her divorce she missed her husband's work events. Unhappy is the woman who has become consumed by her husband's activities at the cost of her own life and identity. If her husband leaves, she will feel she has lost not only a partner but a way of life.

What if you want to talk and your partner is silent, or will not agree that there is anything to talk about? Do you recognize that? I have suggested in the first chapter of this book ways to go about getting your partner to listen to you, but you should also be clear that it is not you who are reluctant to find the words to describe how you are feeling. You might not want to put all the marital cards on the table for fear of the changes to your life that would follow. Make sure that when you do talk to your partner you don't hide the real issues which are worrying you.

Can you find the help you need?

In Chapter Nine I have listed many different Internet sites which offer general legal advice. There is a great deal of free advice available on the web, and if you do not have ready access to a computer it is possible to search the Internet at most public libraries either free or for very little cost. The advantage of doing this is that it is very helpful to look for the information you need in your own time and without having to answer personal questions. You may not feel ready for face-to-face discussions yet. However, you may want to see what kind of help is at hand if you are thinking of leaving or if you sense that it is on the cards that your partner will leave you.

If you are wondering about your legal position and are unclear about your rights, it is a good idea to gather as much data as you can from the start. You may well be pleased later on that you have acted on some of the points which are listed, such as remaking your will. Where possible, I have also listed telephone contact numbers. Remember that although the Internet can be a mine of useful information and help, each case is individual, and so many of the facts given may not apply to you. Be careful, and use sense and caution. For instance, make sure you know the difference between counselling and mediation. It is often easy to confuse them. Mediation has been described as 'assisted decisions', and it is most certainly *not* about taking sides in any dispute. If you see a mediator, you should be aware that it is not an occasion to mend fences, but to reach some agreement about the children. If you want help with trying to mend or recover from a relationship, then see a counsellor, with or without your partner.

If you consider seeking psychological help, then I have listed in detail the different paths you can choose from. The idea of long-term psychotherapy may not appeal to you, and in any case it is not appropriate for everyone. Yet chatting to others on the net, or seeing a counsellor, may be very helpful indeed. If you can think of lightening some of your burdens by talking to a professional you will be in a better position to understand if your children need extra help too.

Try to identify for yourself the different ways in which you are coping (or not) with the stress of a threatened or real break-up. Decide if you need more support. This can be particularly important if you are supporting children who because of the family circumstances show signs of tension.

A divorcing couple

Just as I don't think anyone enters into marriage lightly, I don't believe anyone begins the long road to divorce or separation without a lot of thought either. Of course there are circumstances in which a break-up is inevitable, such as when one partner has a brutal hold on the other. As we have seen, there is growing recognition of the incidence of domestic violence, but even here we should distinguish between a one-off blow and relentless emotional or physical assault. Has there been a gradual change in your partner? Have you considered that he might be suffering from an illness? Is alcohol or drug abuse a factor? Even though part of you may be sympathetic to the unhappiness of your partner, safety for yourself and your children must come first.

> '*I had to leave after years of abuse. I went to the citizen's advice and they told me that because we were not married I would get the children. The next day I went to housing advice and they sent me to a refuge in the Midlands. He found me and tried to snatch the children but I got an injunction. The solicitor at the time was brilliant but the police were not helpful at all.*'

Ask yourself this: if a stranger came up to you and treated you in the way your partner does, what would you do? My hunch is that you would scream for help, and would not stop until you got it. Remember, do not delay. Some women have, with tragic results.

Discovery of infidelity can be compared to a physical attack, and is more than some people can put up with. Is general unhappiness a reason to get divorced? Well, we all have the choice now whether or not to stay married, even though the path of divorce is a thorny one. Maybe it is your partner who wants a divorce, and this leaves you no choice in the matter. But if you are the one to bring about the upheaval, you will know that there is no easy way to tell your partner you are leaving. Unless you have reached a mutual decision, you will have had to think long and hard how to go about this. It can be surprisingly difficult to do. That is why there are men and women who dodge the issue altogether and slip away unannounced. Surely a partner, someone you have loved and with whom you have shared even a few years of your life, deserves more than this. The only reason I can think of which would make this acceptable is where you genuinely believe your life could be in danger if you were to tell your partner face-to-face.

A divorce affects more than just the couple. The family and other guests who danced at your wedding will also be touched deeply by the news and mourn the death of your marriage in one way or another. Be prepared for your parents and your in-laws to be bowled over by the news. Either they will be distressed by the thought of the pain which any divorce brings to the family, and so add to your grief, or they will be quick to tell you that they knew it wouldn't last and that you were foolish to think otherwise. Both reactions are equally hurtful.

The family divorce

If a couple who do not have children decide to go their separate ways, that is sad enough, but it is for them alone to cope with. The picture clouds over considerably when there are children of the marriage. All research indicates that a stable framework is best for children and they thrive better when both parents bring them up. Research also shows that children of cohabitees are twice as likely to see their parents separate as those born within marriage. So even though you have not married, the break-up of your family will be as painful and complicated as if you had. This is only the first part of the scenario, the actual untangling is far worse.

Although children may suffer from living with parents who are at war with each other, a divorce affects them even more deeply. To see a mum or dad move out, which may entail a change of home and school, can contribute to the chaos which divorce brings with it. It may mean a mother has to return to work earlier than planned. A study funded by the Joseph Rowntree Foundation in 2001 found that children whose mother or father stayed at home to look after them did better those whose parents both work. After a divorce there is often no choice. The children may feel they have to choose one parent over another, so that loyalties get stretched to breaking point. I have discussed in Chapter Five ways minimizing the pain for the kids, but the best laid plans do not always come about. Children overhear, or are told, more than they need to know.

If one parent has moved in with a new partner, the one left behind understandably feels angry and hurt. Often these feelings spill over onto the children, who may even be encouraged to stop seeing their other parent. Nothing could be more cruel than to put a child in this position. I do appreciate that when you are hurt it is tempting to lash out, and one way of getting your own back on your departing spouse is to muddy the waters where the children are concerned. This is where it is vitally important to hold back, if you can, to grit your teeth and acknowledge that you should put the children's interests first, so that it is possible for them to keep in touch with the other parent.

It is often in the early days that a departing mother, or father, will think it best to lie low and to contact the children later when they have had a chance to absorb some of the changes. This is a big mistake. Communication should be kept up with the children from day one. Any child needs to be reassured that both parents will still be very involved in his or her life. And they need to see that put into practice at once. Do your best to set up arrangements for the children from the start. They will need to know what is happening, and you may be able to discuss with them what the timing and duration of being with the other parent should be. Parenting is not only about taking the kids to the park, but also about knowing when they need to go to the dentist, what is happening at school, and agreeing on birthday or Christmas gifts for them. Children are smart, so decide together that you will not let them get into the position of telling one parent that, for instance, 'Dad says he will buy it for me.' Refrain from asking the children too many questions about how 'the other half lives' when they are with you, and hope that your ex does the same. Make sure you have told the school, and any others carers, about the change in your children's life.

There are many ways to keep up the communication with a child. Letters, telephone calls, and now a fax or e-mail will keep you in touch. Even very young children like to receive mail. I have spelt out the dangers of Parental Alienation Syndrome in Chapter Five, so beware that you do not become a victim of this, or that you are accused by your ex-partner of encouraging the children to turn their back on him. Remember, when it comes to the care of the children it seems that 'anything goes' and accusations of abuse and neglect frequently become the currency used in divorce. Make sure you do not get involved in these accusations. If the children feel they have been rejected, this feeling will stay with them for a lifetime.

There are tug-of-love children where a parent who has custody decides to move away, perhaps thousands of miles. What is to be done? The law as it stands in the UK looks to the welfare of the parent who has custody, since if he or she is unhappy it will reflect on the child's well-being. This means a parent can move so far away that to all intents and purposes the other parent is cut out of the child's life. I can think of no happy solution in these circumstances. To forbid a parent to return to a country of origin, or to move to where the new husband or wife works or lives would be unreasonable. Yet what of the left-behind parent? More importantly, what of the child? As always it is the child who suffers. In circumstances such as these the fallout and grief is terrible for everybody.

There *are* couples who, although they could not live together, find they can cooperate as parents. In fact I know of some who are more comfortable making arrangements once they are apart, than when they lived together as a couple. There has to be give and take, and flexibility, where the children are concerned. Keep to your part of the bargain and don't expect miracles from your ex-partner. Compromise is often the name of the game, and if that works, why not?

One way to bring about this state of affairs is to let go of blame and resentment towards your ex-partner. If you can find a way to forgive your ex, it will help you to move on. If you are the one who has been left you will have to work on rebuilding your self-esteem, or if you have been the one to flee, you may have to deal with your own feelings of guilt. Holding on to those feelings not only damages the children, but you too. It will make your recovery even harder.

On your own

Have you been able to turn your view of life into a positive one? After the hurt of a divorce, you may be actually enjoying an element of peace in your life. A lull in the rows and fights which you were caught up in before one of you moved out is a welcome reprieve. Madonna's success with her song, 'You'll See' owes a lot to women and men who want to show an ex that they can survive on their own.

You will know that a divorce is more than just a piece of paper, but hopefully the emotional untangling will be well underway by now. Being on your own again, a single person, brings with it an opportunity which is there for the taking. Can you see it as a new phase and one which gives you choices again? The divorce may or may not have been of your making, but either way this is a time to reassess your life. If you are a man, you will probably have an easier entry back into the single life than a woman. Even today an extra man is always welcome at a party, and there should be no shortage of women who are keen to cook a meal for you.

If you have looked at the list of first aid advice on page 66 you should have got into a routine for caring for yourself. It may have come as a horrible shock to you to realize how much of the 'maintenance' of family life your ex was responsible for. You may have had to learn more than you imagined about keeping up the home, or the car, or the pets. On the other hand, orchestrating a house move, sorting out the divorce and understanding your financial position will have brought with it a growing sense of competence and independence.

On the down side, though, you may still be struggling with loneliness. It may have been a shock to discover that there are hours to fill which just seemed to vanish when you had a partner, even though you thought you did nothing for or with each other. Time can hang heavily if you do not like being on your own. You may fear being ill, and anxious that there will be no one to look after you. You may also hate sleeping alone again, and miss an active sex life and not being physically held by anyone. If you are the one to go to a new partner, you may be just as uneasy about all the difficulties which such a huge change has brought about. I have very often heard the cry, 'Why did no one tell me that divorce hurt so much?'

Never again! Really?

During the break-up of a relationship the words 'never again' are often heard. Somehow time begins to alter that and you may find you are looking around for a new love. Make quite sure you are ready. You certainly don't want to jump from the frying pan into the fire. Hopefully you will have made some new friends. It is a splendid idea to mix with people who did not know you when you were part of a couple. They will get to know the 'new' you, and see you as you are now.

Ask yourself if you have taken the time it needs to recover your sense of self, and check to make sure you are not still feeling excessively bruised. If you feel that you are robust enough for the dating game, then have a go. Take care over the kind of people you are attracted to. Do they remind you of your ex? We are often captivated by one type of personality, and if you have not acknowledged that, you will be in danger of making the same mistake again in the choice of partner. Do you feel you have learnt from the past? Those who have not are doomed to repeat it, so be on your guard. If you are blinkered to this it will be your friends and family who are amazed to see history repeat itself. Don't force yourself out into the singles game if it is only to show your ex that you can be loved and be sexually attracted again. It might give you a momentary sense of satisfaction to be wanted once more, but if it doesn't last, the crash, when it comes, will be all the harder to bear.

The strange thing about love is that it often finds us when we are not looking for it. Searching for it doesn't always turn out to be the right way to find it. Desperation to have a new partner can be picked up by others in an unconscious way, and can be very off-putting. So you may well discover that being totally involved in your new way of life or exciting new work, is the quickest route to finding someone to love and who loves you back. Learn from experience, go about life just being your friendly self, show interest in the outside world, and there is every chance that you will love and be loved again.

Marrying second time around

If you are considering a second marriage make sure you are marrying for the right reasons. Be certain that you are not leaping into another marriage because you find the world a cold place to be on your own. We all need intimacy in our lives, but clutching at someone who may or may not be offering what you need is no guarantee of happiness. It can be tempting for a single parent to look, consciously or not, for a mother or father for the children. None of these reasons is a sufficient basis for remarriage.

Have you considered a pre-nuptial agreement this time? Much publicity was given to the contract entered into between the film stars Michael Douglas and Catherine Zeta Jones. Mr Douglas had just emerged from a very costly divorce, but what caught the attention of the press was a $5 million 'fling' penalty for Mr Douglas if he strays. Although a pre-nuptial agreement is not legally binding in the UK couples can and do make an agreement about who has what in the event of a break-up. With many women now being high earners this is a two-way street. The romantic ones among us may feel that considering such an arrangement in advance suggests that a divorce is on the cards, but having seen the agony that some couples go through when dividing property and assets, there is something to be said for being level headed, even when selecting the orange blossom for the wedding.

If you are marrying someone who has been married before, or it is the second time for you, then the wedding is likely to be a different experience from the first time. Not second best, but different. One issue may be where you will be married. Today there is much more choice as many different venues are now licensed for marriages, and a good place to search for these is on the Internet. You may even be able to marry in church. The Chester Diocese has become the first in England to permit divorcees with a former spouse still living to remarry in church. All forty-three dioceses are voting on the issue and eleven have so far come out in favour. The others are waiting for General Synod approval.

As we saw in Chapter Seven, care needs to be taken over the others affected by the wedding. This will span the generations, as your parents and future parents-in-law will have their own feelings about this occasion. There is likely to be an ex in the background, especially if there are children around. The reactions of the children to meeting a future partner of a parent has been discussed already and careful planning about meeting up with the children, and then their role at the wedding, must be coordinated like a military operation. The way these events are organized will have repercussions down the years.

A double dose of parenting?

Few are likely to take on the parenting of someone else's children without a great deal of thought and heart-searching, but when a couple fall in love it is all too easy to hope the children will join in this making of a new family with joy and delight. We know that it is not always the case. Many a stepparent finds himself or herself at sea for quite some time. With the best will in the world it can be very hard to be friendly and loving to children who do not want a friend, or to be loved! If you add to that the complication that you may both have children from an earlier relationship, then you have an explosive mixture of emotions.

When a couple decide to have a baby, they know that they are in for a time of upheaval and change. However, most couples settle down with their new child and getting to know their baby brings a couple very close as they unite to become parents. In this way they bond together as a family in a loving way. But having a ready-made family of children who might well not want to blend together, or who have different allegiances, can put a colossal strain on a new relationship. It is an awkward situation for any stepparent when there are children who come and go between their biological parents and the new stepfamily. This can bring about a burden which may not have been anticipated.

> 'I have to say my children from my first marriage were impossible. They would come and really upset my stepchildren. I know, I know, they were struggling with it all. But it came down to having to choose, and I chose my new family.'

This was a particularly sad ending to a divorce where previously the parents had successfully managed shared parenting for three years. When Ted remarried and became a stepfather the balance was lost and even with all the adults of one mind, the children would not settle in Ted's new home. Ted came to the conclusion that trying to blend them, even at weekends and holidays, was impossible and he stopped seeing his son and daughter. Ted's story shows that no matter how long after the break-up of the original family, introducing new relationships can skew the status quo, so be aware of the dangers lurking around in the shadows.

Children born into a parent's second family have a lot to cope with too. There may be half-brothers and half-sisters coming and going. Their lifestyle may be penalized because of the financial obligations a parent has to support other children, and perhaps a first wife or husband. Spare a thought, too, for how hard it must be if a parent disappears from time to time to visit with other children.

> 'My parents didn't even try to make us a blended family. I don't know why. Once or twice we were all together, but usually my dad went off every other weekend. It wasn't talked about, but my sister and I knew he had gone to see his boys. We hated it.'
>
> 'Looking back my sister and I were very naughty. We blamed our horrible step for taking Dad away from us and Mum. We did everything we could to be difficult. In the end we lost out because they wouldn't have anything to do with us. We were only kids though.'

Let's not be left with the picture of destructive, delinquent step-children. It is hard to be a stepchild. I have heard this sentiment expressed more than once: 'I visit Mum and Kevin, and I visit Dad and Moira, I visit my two lots of grandparents too. But where do I live?' Think about that. Think also, about the children who spend a great deal of their life on the road, or in airports. The arrangements for the children you have agreed with your ex might look good on paper but pay special attention to your children to see whether all the travelling and changes get them down. I have met many children who sigh and remind me that they always seem to be saying 'goodbye' to someone. If you have moved away from where your children live, are you able to arrange to do a large part of the travelling? Consider this.

A Scottish teenager was reported (*The Times*, 5 March 2001) to be suing his father for money to help to fund him through university. Paul is taking his father to court to seek maintenance to support him during his four-year degree course. His parents were separated five years before and were divorced in 1999. Paul, who lives with his mother, claims that his father cut him and his two sisters off after they had snubbed his new girlfriend. This story is just one example of the multitude of family feuds which go on and on after a divorce.

If you are a stepparent, do take heart that there *are* happy and settled stepfamilies around. If you are agonizing over the making of your family do get help of the kind suggested in Chapter Nine. Don't become part of another step- or blended family that did not make it. There is an awful lot at stake.

Family life after divorce

We have seen that you don't have to have been married to suffer through a 'divorce'. If you have cohabited, the break-up can be just as painful. Although some people think that cohabitation is a preparation for marriage, or a trial run, there is no evidence to support the hope that if a couple do then marry, they will live happily ever after. Statistics show that the longer the cohabitation before marriage, the greater the likelihood of divorce. Those who marry after the birth of their first child run a specially high risk of divorce. So, cohabitation does nothing to strengthen marriages, and indeed is associated with an increased risk of marital breakdown. If we look at cohabitations that do not go on to marriage, they are about four times more likely to break down than marriages. In her book *Marriage-Lite* Patricia Morgan spells out all the difficulties couples face if they cohabit, and that those with children who cohabit are even more vulnerable.

If you are on your own after a divorce, then take some time to be happy. You deserve it. Don't keep looking back over your shoulder at better times. By all means remember them, but it will not help you to keep ruminating over why your marriage collapsed. You should have thought through why this happened, so draw a line under it, and move on. Use this new understanding of yourself when you look for a new partner in time. Meanwhile, go for experiences in life which you can enjoy. Break new ground and try to restore your sense of identity and belief in yourself. If you are a single parent, this still applies to you, although it may be more difficult as you have to keep contact with your ex because of the children. This means that you are constantly reminded of your earlier married life. However, try to distinguish between your role as a parent, and your own single life. In the periods when the children are with their other parent, use the time to your advantage.

You may hate to hear this, especially if you are the one who has been left by your partner, but time will help you to feel less pain. You will be a star when you can reach the point of politeness and civility with your ex. Remember, there was love there once between you, and if only for the sake of the children try to get some kind of relationship going which does not cause you heartache each time you meet. As parents, you are in for a long haul and one day you may even be able to dance together at your child's wedding.

If you are a parent who no longer lives with the children, then your life will have altered considerably. You may or may not have moved on to a new partner but, in any event, planning shared parenting will take some organization. Hopefully you will have realized that children do need two parents who are both active in their lives, but you may feel you are drowning in a pool of schedules and timetables. If your new partner has children too the required organization multiplies many times. Building a family is never easy and establishing a second family is especially hard. There is no other way to say it. A step- or blended family will have the problems which all families have, with more added. You will be faced by decisions such as where to celebrate the children's birthdays: at your house, or the other parent's; whether to celebrate twice: is that good for the child, and will the best friend come to both; and a thousand other issues of supreme importance.

Remember that whether you like it or not, when you become a stepparent you assume a very important role in a child's life. Try to see each event through the children's eyes, and above all, *talk* to them. It is important for every family to spend time together, but it is even more so if you are trying to blend a family together. Don't believe that at the first falling-out everything is lost. Don't think that every row a child has with a parent is caused by the family situation. Don't assume the worst. Remember, it is never too late to mend fences.

We know that families come in all shapes and sizes, and yours is no exception. After any divorce all the pieces are up in the air, and how they will be reassembled depends on many factors. Some of you are almost certainly still walking wounded, so you need time to recover. All you can do is your best. Don't assume you know what either your partner, ex-partner or children are thinking. You, more than anyone, know what a broken relationship can mean, so make sure that lightning doesn't strike twice. Take care of what you have got.

Over the rainbow

Finding your way through divorce is never easy and cannot be pain free, but whether it is something which was thrust upon you, or was your choice, you will have discovered there are many bridges to cross. Although at times it may have seemed very hard, and it was often difficult to glimpse a light at the end of the tunnel, I hope you did not feel alone. Some of the suggestions and strategies I have listed may have helped and encouraged you, and I trust you can now believe that there is life after divorce.

Although no one would willingly go through the break-up of a relationship and all that it entails, you may have learnt more about yourself in the process. The skill is to learn from the past, and the present, and to go on learning. We all acquire our knowledge about life from experience, so build on this awareness, and seize any second chance you have for happiness. Don't block out all the memories of your marriage. Remember you were happy together once. Let this help you keep a grip on your post-separation relationship, which is especially important if you need to work together as parents.

As you gather your strength you can move onto centre stage again, and become a major player. You know now that happy marriages don't just happen, but have to be made to happen. You know the formula: Love? Certainly. Trust? Of course. A determination to succeed? Naturally. A little bit of luck? To be sure. And a belief in each other. Get the mixture right, and if you have the chance, choose wisely. You and any new partner can have a happy life together and even share the same dreams for the future. With your new-found ability to see the different facets which make a loving relationship survive, the future should look rosy.

About my website

www.familyonwards.com began as an Internet help and support site for parents and grandparents of divorce. Over the year or so that it has been on-line I have heard from a large number of men, women and children who want information about other relationship issues as well.

There are now over 100 articles to read on the site. They cover marriage, second weddings, domestic violence, gay family issues, stepparenting, single parenting, blended families and more. Books and videos of particular interest to parents, families and people caring for children with special needs are regularly reviewed on the site.

The 'Article of the Month', which usually covers an issue of relevance to the time of year or something currently in the news, is one of the site's more popular features. There are also links through to many other worthwhile sites for parents, grandparents and children.

Do come and visit www.familyonwards.com.

Further reading

Cross, Penny, *Lost Children, A Guide for Separating Parents*, Velvet Glove Publishing, London, 2000.

Curtis, Jill *Making and Breaking Families: The Way Ahead for Parents and their Children*, Free Association Books, London, 1998.

Curtis, Jill, and Ellis, Virginia, *Where's Daddy? Separation and Your Child*, Bloomsbury, London, 1996.

Kohner, Nancy, and Henley, Alix, *When a Baby Dies*, Routledge, London, 2001.

Kuriansky, Dr Judy, *The Complete Idiot's Guide to A Healthy Relationship*, Alpha Books, New York, 1998.

McGee, Caroline, *Childhood Experiences of Domestic Violence*, Jessica Kingsley Publishers, London, 2000.

Morgan, Patricia, *Marriage-Lite: The Rise of Cohabitation and its Consequences*, Institute for the Study of Civil Society, London, 2000.

Moulder, Christine, *Miscarriage: Woman's Experiences and Needs*, Routledge, London, 2001.

Phillips, Melanie, *The Sex-change Society, Feminised Britain and the Neutered Male*, The Social Market Foundation, London, 1999.

Secker, Sue, *The Families Need Fathers Guide for Separating Parents*, Families Need Fathers Publications, London, 2001.

Wallerstein, Judith, and Lewis, Julia, and Blakeslee, Sandra, *The Unexpected Legacy of Divorce*, Hyperion Books, New York, 2000.

Watchel, Dr Ellen, *We Love each Other, But . . .*, Golden Books, New York, 1999.

Wyon, Linda, *Ben's Story: An Introduction to Contact Centres*, National Association of Child Contact Centres, Nottingham, 1999.

Index